Weekend Projects for Your
Mustang 2005–Today

By Dan Sanchez and Drew Phillips

First published in 2010 by Motorbooks, an imprint of MBI
Publishing Company, 400 First Avenue North, Suite 300,
Minneapolis, MN 55401 USA

Motorbooks titles are also available at discounts in bulk
quantity for industrial or sales-promotional use. For details
write to Special Sales Manager at MBI Publishing Company,
400 First Avenue North, Suite 300, Minneapolis, MN
55401 USA.

To find out more about our books, join us online at
www.motorbooks.com.

ISBN-13: 978-0-7603-3685-4

President/CEO: Ken Fund
Publisher: Zack Miller
Editor: Peter Schletty
Creative Director: Michele Lanci-Altomare
Design Manager: James Kegley
Designer: Danielle Smith

Printed in China

Contents

Introduction

Since it hit showroom floors in 1964, the Ford Mustang has always represented one of the best performance bargains money could buy. More than 45 years and 9 million Mustangs later, Ford's pony car still maintains the tradition of exceptional performance at an affordable price.

Perhaps the Mustang's most appealing attribute to car enthusiasts is that it can be easily modified to fit one's personal taste. Owners can add performance parts to go faster, body kits, wheels, or even paint jobs, as well as any number of accessories to ensure that their Mustangs are one of a kind. This especially holds true for the latest generation Mustang that was introduced in 2005, with dozens of aftermarket companies producing hundreds of parts that allow owners to customize their cars in countless ways. It is for this reason that the Specialty Equipment Market Association (SEMA) named the 2005-and-later Mustang the most customizable car on the market today, citing that 46 percent of owners begin modifying their cars within three weeks of ownership.

It is with this in mind that we wrote *Weekend Projects for Your Mustang 2005–Today*. We hope that if you own a modern Mustang and want to learn more about customizing and modifying your car, you will be able to learn not only what parts are available for it but also what it takes to install them. We have tried to cover all the bases, from changing the simplest items like an air intake system to difficult projects like adding a complete supercharger kit. Whether your Mustang is a daily driver or a weekend show car, we hope this book will inspire you to spend many happy hours in your garage creating your dream pony car.

SECTION 1
ENGINE

PROJECT 1
Air Intake Upgrade

 Increasing airflow to the Mustang's V-8

 Time: 1 hour

S **Cost:** $289.99

 Skill level: Easy; bolt-on with no modifications

 Tools: No special tools; requires flat screwdriver, 8mm and 10mm socket wrench, and 2.5mm Allen wrench

Modifying the air intake system is one of the easiest and cheapest ways to gain additional horsepower on your 2005-and-later Mustang. Most aftermarket systems utilize an open air element and a larger intake tube that allow more air to reach the engine. Intakes can vary in the types of materials used, and which one you choose mostly comes down to personal preference. Some systems also require the Mustang's computer system to be retuned, in which case you will need a programmer as well. To make the most of any intake system, we would recommend pairing it with a programmer whether the manufacturer requires it or not. Look for retailers that offer intake systems packaged with a programmer that has a tune calibrated to a specific air intake manufacturer. With this combination you should expect a gain of 15 to 25 additional horsepower at the rear wheels.

For our application, we used a BBK Performance cold air intake system constructed of a CNC-machined, powder-coated aluminum casting that comes in a titanium, chrome, or charcoal metallic finish. The kit also comes with a heat shroud that surrounds a conical air filter, which can be washed and reused for the lifetime of the vehicle. BBK claims a gain of 15 horsepower and 25 lbs-ft of torque at the rear wheels with the addition of this intake system.

SOURCE
BBK Performance
27440 Bostik Ct.
Temecula, CA 92590
(951) 296-1771
www.bbkperformance.com

1

Start by disconnecting the negative battery terminal. Remove the stock intake tube by unbolting the hose clamp that connects it to the throttle body and airbox.

2

Disconnect the PCV hose from the side of the intake tube by twisting the green locking clip and pulling it away from the inlet hose. Then remove the intake tube from the engine bay.

3

Unplug the mass air meter from the tube going into the airbox by sliding the red locking clip back. Then squeeze the tab while pulling it away.

4

Remove the bolt near the fender that holds the stock airbox in place.

5

Once the bolt is removed, remove the stock airbox from the engine bay.

6

Remove the fasteners that hold the radiator cover in place by gently prying the center of each plastic rivet out with a screwdriver.

7

Once all of the fasteners have been removed, lift the radiator cover up and set it aside.

8 Unbolt the plate that holds down the radiator on the driver's side. Once removed, set it aside for later.

9 Place the BBK intake shroud into the engine bay and align the holes with those on the fender and near the radiator.

10 With the holes aligned, bolt the shroud in place.

11 Bolt in the plate that holds down the radiator, this time with the intake shroud fitted underneath.

12 Reinstall the radiator cover by simply pushing the fasteners back in place.

13 Remove the mass air sensor from the stock airbox by unscrewing it and pulling it straight out.

ENGINE

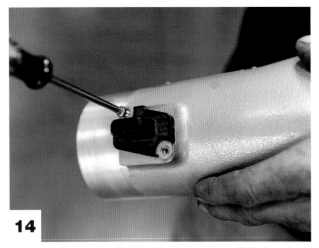

14 Bolt the mass air sensor into the BBK intake tube using the supplied screws.

15 Place the blue coupler hose and the hose clamps over the intake tube and install it by fitting the hose over the throttle body.

16 Secure the hose over the throttle body and adjust the hose clamps so that one fits over the intake tube and the other over the throttle body.

17 Place the air filter inside the airbox and connect it to the intake tube. Once it is in place, tighten the hose clamp to secure it.

18 Tighten the hose clamps around the intake tube and the throttle body.

19 Reconnect the PCV tube to the BBK intake, then reconnect the mass air meter and negative battery terminal. The installation is complete.

ENGINE

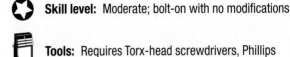

PROJECT 2
Throttle Body Upgrade

? Even more airflow

Time: 1–2 hours

$ Cost: $299.99

★ Skill level: Moderate; bolt-on with no modifications

Tools: Requires Torx-head screwdrivers, Phillips screwdriver, and 8mm and 10mm socket wrenches

The 2005-and-later Mustang features an electronically controlled dual throttle body that does an excellent job of metering air into the intake manifold. Of course, more air is better, and several aftermarket companies have developed throttle bodies with larger openings that can feed more air into the Mustang GT's 4.6-liter V-8.

BBK Performance in Temecula, California, specializes in throttle body applications and has developed a 62mm unit for 2005-and-later Mustangs. The unit is CNC machined from 356 aluminum castings and is designed to increase flow over 30 percent compared to the stock throttle body. At a retail price of $299.99, the BBK 62mm throttle body is a relatively cost effective way to add horsepower. BBK claims that independent dyno tests have yielded gains of approximately 15 horsepower and 20 lbs-ft of torque on an otherwise stock Mustang.

The installation is relatively simple and involves removing the stock intake tube and throttle body, transferring some of the components from the stock throttle body to the BBK unit, and then reinstalling. In some cases, the "check engine" light can come on, in which case the voltage of the throttle position sensor needs to be adjusted. BBK has detailed instructions and a video on the company's website showing how to adjust the voltage, as well as full installation instructions.

SOURCE

BBK Performance
27440 Bostik Ct.
Temecula, CA 92590
(951) 296-1771
www.bbkperformance.com

ENGINE

The BBK 62mm throttle body is CNC machined from 356 aluminum castings and increases airflow to the engine without the need for tuning.

1 Start by disconnecting the battery. Next, disconnect the positive crankcase ventilation hose (PCV) connection from the air intake tube.

2 Disconnect the mass air meter connection by releasing the locking tabs and pulling them away from the intake system.

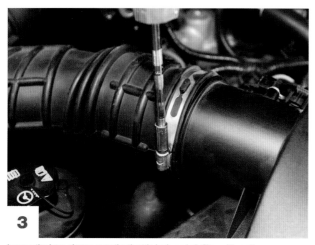

3 Loosen the hose clamps near the throttle body and air filter with an 8mm socket wrench.

4 Once the clamps are loosened, remove the air intake tube and set it aside.

5 Disconnect the throttle position sensor (TPS) from the left side of the throttle body by pulling back on the red locking clips and squeezing the connectors while pulling them away.

6 Disconnect the electric motor harnesses from the right side of the throttle body by pulling back on the red locking clips and squeezing the connectors while pulling them away.

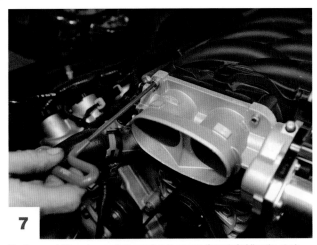

7 Use 8mm and 10mm long socket wrenches to remove the nuts holding the stock throttle body in place. This one has been removed before and uses hex-head bolts as a replacement for the stock studs.

8 Remove the throttle body from the intake manifold. The stock O-ring behind it will be reused.

9 Unscrew the TPS sensor from the throttle body using a Torx wrench. Be sure to pull it straight off, and do not twist the insides or it might break.

10 Bolt the TPS sensor onto the BBK throttle body with the two factory screws.

11 Remove the perimeter screws from the electric motor housing using a Phillips screwdriver.

12 Once unbolted, remove the electric motor housing from the stock throttle body.

13

Once the electric motor housing is removed, the plastic cap spring will uncoil. Be careful not to lose it.

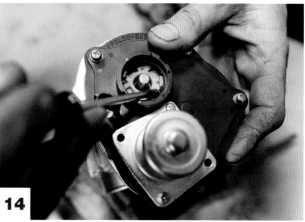

14

Fit the plastic cap spring and the electric motor housing cover onto the BBK throttle body and loosely bolt it on. Once this is done, the plastic cap spring needs to be rotated. There are tabs on the plastic cap spring that need to line up with landings in the motor housing cover. To achieve this, use a screwdriver to rotate the spring cap counterclockwise approximately 180 degrees until they line up. If this is done correctly, the throttle body should snap shut on its own after being opened manually.

15

Once the throttle body is working correctly, bolt the electric motor housing cover down completely.

16

The BBK throttle body is now ready to be installed in your Mustang. Be sure to plug in the TPS sensor and electric motor harnesses.

Reinstall the intake tube and tighten the hose clamps. Then plug in the PCV connection and mass airflow sensor. Finally, reconnect the battery to complete the installation.

17

ENGINE

PROJECT 3
Adding a Supercharger

 Blown away

 Time: 14–20 hours

Cost: $6,000

Skill level: Experienced

Tools: Requires special fuel line removal tool and 5mm hex-head T-wrench included in kit; uses standard and metric SAE socket wrench set, Sawzall or cutting wheel, and drill

Throughout the years, Mustangs and supercharging have seemed to go hand in hand. With the introduction of the S197 models, that relationship hasn't changed. A variety of Mustangs come off the showroom floor outfitted with a variety of superchargers. Such builders as Shelby, Roush, Saleen, and more use supercharging to obtain 150 horsepower or more from the 4.6-liter or 5.4-liter V-8 engines. But you don't need to buy a complete car just to get the same kind of power. With the right kit, your 4.6-liter V-8 can make as much as 450–480 rear-wheel horsepower that can be easily driven on the street.

While installation takes a lot of time and patience, a supercharger kit can be installed over a weekend, but you need to be experienced enough to follow the manufacturer's directions. Most of the installation time is spent re-routing portions of the factory wiring, engine, and relocating the alternator and ECU to make room for a new intercooled intake and the supercharger unit.

We elected to use Kenne Bell 2.8-liter supercharger kit No. TS-10005-INT. It produces 8–10 psi of boost on a stock 4.6-liter V-8, enough to give this engine 482 rear-wheel

horsepower at only 9 psi of boost. In addition, the twin-screw design offers lower air inlet temperatures from a very efficient design. Higher efficiency requires less horsepower to drive the impellers, and in this case the 2.8-liter supercharger uses 56 horsepower less than most other blower designs currently found on Roush, Saleen, Shelby, and GT-500 models.

Obviously we can't cover a complete installation in one small section of this book, but we've outlined some of the major points of what's involved with the installation of a supercharger like this. If you take your time and install the kit by following the instructions and carefully checking each connection and modification, you'll end up with a powerful Mustang that still gets 17 miles per gallon for city driving but that's a blast to drive and well worth the investment.

SOURCE
Kenne Bell Superchargers
10743 Bell Court
Rancho Cucamonga, CA 91730
(909) 941-6646
www.kennebell.net

ENGINE

There's nothing like a Mustang with a blower under the hood. Adding a supercharger can turn your ordinary Mustang into a menacing street machine while still maintaining its fuel economy and driving pleasure.

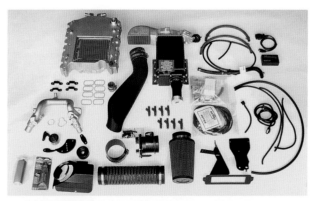
A kit like this one includes a ton of components, but if you take your time and follow the instructions, it's actually not too difficult for an experienced backyard mechanic to install a supercharger.

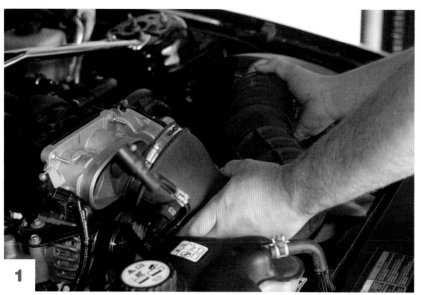

Start by unhooking the battery terminals and removing the air intake system, throttle body, and linkage.

The fuel system will have to be removed. The Kenne Bell kit comes with the fuel line removal tool to detach the fuel lines from the engine's fuel rail system.

The factory fuel rails are unbolted and removed from each side of the engine. The fuel injectors will also be replaced with higher-flow units.

With all hoses and connections removed, the factory intake manifold is unbolted from the engine.

With the intake removed, you have access to some of the cooling lines and factory wiring harness.

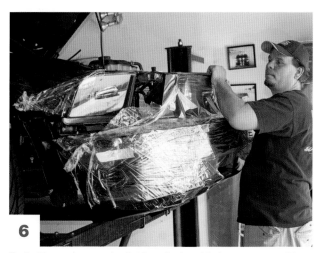

6

The front bumper is wrapped so that it won't get scratched once you remove it to make room for the air intake duct and heat exchanger.

7

With the bumper out of the way, the installation of the Kenne Bell components can take place.

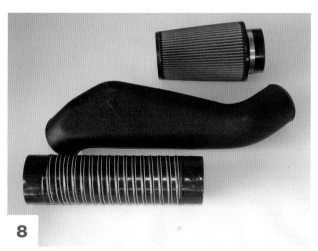

8

A new air intake duct and filter will be routed to the passenger side and take cold air from under the bumper.

9

Here you can see where the radiator core support was trimmed to accommodate the new air duct and filter.

10

In this kit, the factory mass air flow (MAF) sensor will be replaced with a larger 92mm MAF sensor that will fit inline with the air intake duct. Here are what the air intake and MAF sensor look like installed. They will take cold air from outside the engine compartment to improve power.

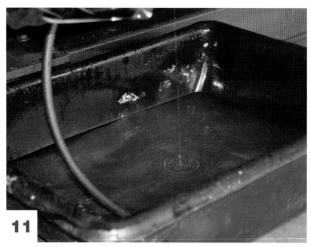

11 All of the engine's cooling fluid is then drained from the petcock on the radiator.

12 The cooling lines are removed from the factory cooling crossover assembly.

13 The factory coolant crossover assembly is replaced with another assembly that features tubing that sits lower in the engine's lifter valley.

14 A new alternator relocation bracket is also installed to make room for the intercooled intake manifold and supercharger.

15 A heat exchanger and coolant reservoir are included in the kit to cool the air intake charge into the intercooled intake manifold.

16 The heat exchanger and pump are mounted in front of the radiator to receive cold air that will provide a much more substantial cooling effect compared to the factory engine cooling system.

ENGINE

17

To make room for a re-routed pulley system, the factory ECU is relocated to the side of the engine compartment.

18

Portions of the wiring harness are opened up to extend the wiring. This allows room for the new MAF sensor and other items that are attached to the factory harness.

19

In order to provide enough fuel under boost, Kenne Bell uses a pump booster that is mounted in the trunk and attaches to the factory fuel pump wiring harness.

20

New 39-pound.injectors are included in the kit and are used in place of the factory units.

21

Kenne Bell designed a new intake manifold with an intercooler inserted inside. Because of the separate heat exchanger and coolant, colder air inlet temperatures will make this system more efficient and make more boost.

22

Once the intake manifold is bolted in place and all the cooling lines are attached, the 2.8-liter supercharger is bolted on top.

ENGINE

All of the wiring, hoses, and air intake system are attached, and the installation is completed.

23

Kenne Bell provides new ECU calibration that's downloaded to provide proper fuel and ignition timing curves to operate the engine with the supercharger.

24

The dyno tests on this kit with only 9 psi of boost made 478.6 horsepower and 451.9 lbs-ft of torque at the rear wheels. This translates to about 550 horsepower at the crank, making this 4.6-liter Mustang more powerful than a stock GT-500.

25

PROJECT 4
Bolting On a Nitrous Oxide System

 Bottle feeding your pony

 Time: 3 hours

Cost: $650–$700

 Skill level: Easy to moderate; basic wiring techniques and experience with AN fittings are a must

 Tools: No special tools; requires Teflon paste, wire cutters, and wire splicers

Nitrous oxide is one of the few performance products that can give your stock 4.6-liter V-8 75–100 extra horsepower without affecting your engine's fuel economy or daily driving experience when it is not in use. Nitrous is a safe and effective way of getting instant horsepower, just as long as you stick to the manufacturer's recommendations regarding the amount and levels of nitrous oxide that you inject into your engine.

We've used nitrous oxide on everything from 1,100-horsepower big-blocks to 200-horsepower V-6 street engines, and when installed correctly, it can give you many years of safe and economical performance. For a street-driven Mustang GT, we found the NOS No. 02121NOS wet nitrous oxide system to be a great method of gaining 75-plus horsepower on a stock engine. This wet system injects both nitrous oxide and fuel into the air inlet duct, a mixture that is sucked into the combustion chamber to increase the engine's compression, which results in more power.

Installation is simple but requires you to follow the instructions carefully, especially when attaching the system's wiring. While the kit comes with all the necessary wire and connectors, make sure that you carefully plan out and route your wiring before making any cuts. It's also a good idea to get some black wire loom to protect the wiring and to keep your engine bay looking neat and clean.

SOURCE

NOS
Holley Performance Products Inc.
1801 Russellville Road
P.O. Box 10360
Bowling Green, KY 42102
(866) G0-HOLLEY

ENGINE

The NOS kit from Holley (No. 02121NOS) includes everything you need to add 75-plus horsepower to a stock 4.6-liter V-8 Mustang.

1

The nitrous oxide bottle is mounted in the trunk using brackets that are drilled and bolted to the trunk floor. A nitrous feed line must extend from the bottle, through one of the trunk access plugs, and along the frame up into the engine. Make sure that it doesn't interfere with the exhaust, steering, suspension, etc.

2

Because the nitrous and fuel will be injected into the intake, disconnect the rubber intake tube from the throttle body and the air filter box.

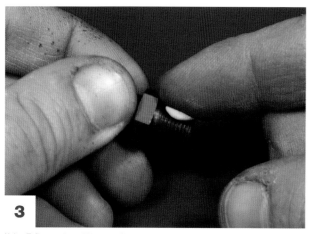

3

Using Teflon paste, not tape, apply some to the threads of the AN fittings that will be attached to the nitrous and fuel solenoids.

4

The solenoids are marked "IN" and "OUT." The fittings screw into the "IN" side of each solenoid.

5

Attach the fittings to the solenoids and tighten with a wrench. The fittings and lines are color coordinated; the blue fittings are for the nitrous oxide while the red are for the fuel.

6

The stainless braided hoses are also color identified and are attached to the "OUT" side of the solenoids.

7 This is what the solenoids should look like with the AN fittings and hoses attached.

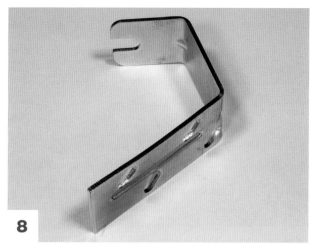

8 A bracket is provided to secure the solenoids to the engine and hold them in place.

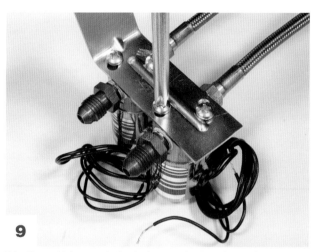

9 Using the provided screws, the bracket is mounted to the underside of the solenoids as shown here.

10 To access pressurized fuel, the fuel pressure sensor must be unbolted from the fuel rail and set aside.

11 A fuel block is added in between the pressure sensor and the rail, allowing fuel to be plumbed to the solenoid. Note the use of the red AN fitting already inserted into the block with Teflon paste.

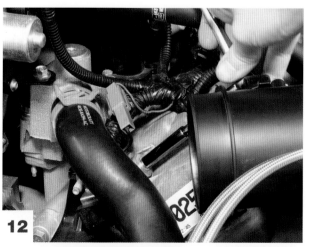

12 The solenoids must be securely mounted to the engine. Unbolt one of the valve cover bolts to hold the bracket in place.

13 Here you can see the orientation of the solenoids and how the bracket secures them in this location.

14 The fuel line is then attached from the solenoid to the block on the fuel rail. The fittings should be tightened using a wrench on the solenoid fitting and one on the fuel line fitting.

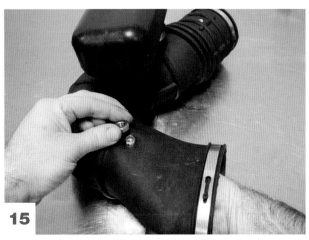

15 Drill a small hole in the underside of the rubber factory inlet tube for the nozzle bung. Following the instructions, place the fitting only a few inches from the front of the throttle body.

16 The NOS nozzle is then attached to the inlet tube bung. Make sure this is tight and leak free because damage can occur if the bung or nozzle leaks.

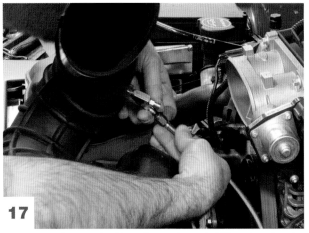

17 The outlet lines from the solenoids are then attached to the NOS nozzle, and the air inlet duct is reattached to the throttle body and the air filter box.

18 Here you can see how the NOS nozzle attaches to the air inlet tube from the underside.

19

The electronics on the NOS kit are easy to set. The two switches on the right are preset to turn the unit on when the throttle position sensor reads 4.3 volts, indicating it is at wide-open throttle. The switches on the left are set to turn the nitrous on at 3,000 rpms and off at 6,000 rpms. We recommend not adjusting the switches and leaving them on the preset settings.

20

Following the instructions, you connect the NOS wiring to the positive side of the battery terminal, a good ground, the throttle position sensor, and a coil trigger that's located on one of the injector wires.

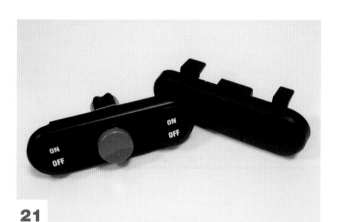

21

The kit also comes with this plug-in switch plate that fits directly in the accessory panel of the factory dash. If your Mustang came fully equipped with the control switches for the information center on the factory gauges, you'll have to find another location for the switches.

22

In this application, we popped off the blank accessory plates on the dash, wired the switches according to the instructions, and popped the NOS switch panel into place.

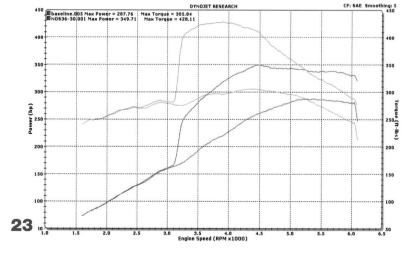

23

On the dyno, the addition of the NOS system yielded nearly 62 additional peak rear-wheel horsepower and an additional 122 lbs-ft of peak torque.

PROJECT 5
Installing a Water/Methanol Injection System

 Make more power and better fuel economy

Time: 1–2 hours

Cost: $720

 Skill level: Moderate to easy; requires some knowledge of air-style compression tubing and fittings

Tools: Drilling required; no special tools

Gas isn't what it used to be. Octane levels decrease as prices keep increasing. Mustang owners look to find ways to save fuel and get the most power from their normally aspirated or supercharged engines. One method that has long been used by turbocharger manufacturers to eliminate detonation and maintain full ignition timing is water/methanol injection.

The process delivers a precise amount of water and methanol that cools combustion temperatures to allow full ignition timing. This allows the engine to make more power and use less fuel. Under boost or higher rpms, the system utilizes a sophisticated computer controller that monitors engine functions and delivers a super-fine mist into the intake system.

Fuel economy gains of 5–10 percent have been documented with slight increases in horsepower without any other changes. For supercharged and high-compression engines, water/methanol injection also allows the engine to run with lower-octane fuel, saving money and allowing the unit to pay for itself over time.

We installed a Snow Performance MPG-Max G System on a normally aspirated Mustang GT. This system can also work on a supercharged engine and features a 2D digital controller and display module, high-power pump, and water/methanol reservoir to easily bolt on to your Mustang and gain some noticeable results.

SOURCE

Snow Performance
1017-A East Hwy 24
Woodland Park, CO 80863
(719) 633-3811
www.SnowPerformance.net

The Snow Performance MPG-Max G System can be used in both normally aspirated and supercharged applications. It comes with a dash-mounted monitor and digital controller featuring 2D mapping, installation hardware, and high-pressure pump. The tank shown here is available if you don't want to use your factory windshield washer reservoir.

ENGINE

In this application, we'll be using the factory windshield washer reservoir, which is unbolted, and the wiring harness to the pump is unplugged.

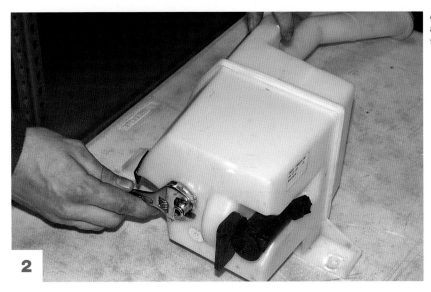

A hole was drilled at the bottom of the reservoir to attach a bulkhead fitting that will be used to deliver fluid to the pump.

The same was done for the fluid level sensor, which is attached near the bottom of the reservoir.

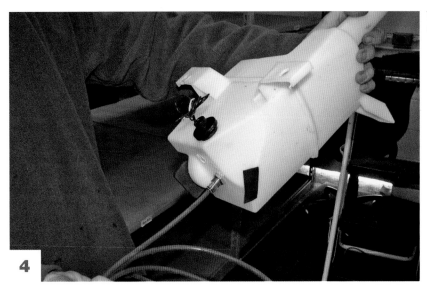

The tubing is inserted into the fitting, and the reservoir is ready to be reinstalled into the Mustang's engine bay.

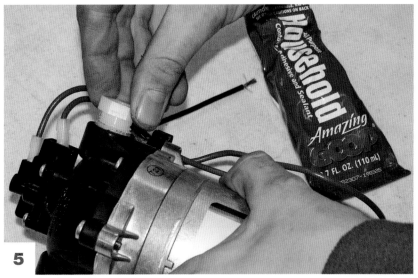

The tube fittings are mounted to the high-pressure pump and are sealed using silicone.

The pump is mounted with the provided hardware. Here you can see how the pump and reservoir fit nicely in the Mustang's engine compartment. The wiring is left loose for now until the rest of the system is installed.

In this application, we are installing the injection system into the intake duct of this Mustang. It would be the same for a supercharged application.

Two holes are drilled for the injection nozzle bungs that will squirt fluid into the intake tract, just before the throttle body.

The injection nozzles and elbows are installed, and the intake can be replaced onto the engine.

ENGINE

31

The tubing is routed from the reservoir to the pump, then to the two nozzles on the intake. The wiring is also gathered together to route through and ultimately end up under the dash.

Here you can see the nozzles connected to the tubing. A nice and clean installation.

The wires from the controller are routed so that they end up under the dash. They will be pushed through the factory rubber grommet to connect to the wiring on the engine side.

13 With the wires running from the engine and up into the controller that's mounted on the dash, the rest of the wiring is connected to a 12-volt ignition power source, ground, and to the pumps. The instructions show how to accomplish this, and all of the wiring connectors are included in the kit.

14 Our Mustang was run on the dyno to test the results of using water/methanol injection. After careful measurement of fuel levels after each run, we measured up to a 10 percent improvement in fuel economy from installing the Snow Performance injection system.

PROJECT 6
Installing an Aftermarket Ignition Coil and Colder Spark Plugs

 Sparking some interest

 Time: 1.5 hours

S **Cost:** Spark plugs (set of 8), $130; coil set (8), $400

 Skill level: Easy; anyone can do it

 Tools: Requires a 9⁄16 spark plug socket wrench or standard 9⁄16 long socket wrench, spark plug gapping tool

ENGINE

Both the 4.6-liter and 5.4-liter Mustang engines that are upgraded with a supercharger, a turbo, or nitrous oxide typically require additional spark energy to fire properly under boost. A popular method to improve the performance of a forced-induction engine is to upgrade to an aftermarket set of coils and move to a colder set of spark plugs.

An aftermarket coil can deliver higher voltage that can improve spark energy and saturation time (recovery time after firing) for higher rpm use. A colder spark plug will help prevent detonation, allowing the engine's computer to allow for maximum timing for increased power under boost.

We used an MSD Blaster coil set that improved saturation time, allowing our engine to get a consistent amount of voltage at higher rpms. In addition, we also upgraded to a set of Brisk 3VR14S Silver spark plugs that have a fine wire center electrode that allows for more room between the insulator and the electrode to induce spark. For forced-induction engines, this is crucial in providing high strength and a dependable spark. Another advantage of the Brisk Silver spark plugs over the popular Autolite HTO is that the Brisk plugs can be gapped to .032–.035 inch, which is recommended when moving up to a spark plug that's one or two steps colder. The HTO cannot be gapped unless you bend the one-piece electrode in the center, which may not be accurate and may cause fouling or a slight misfire.

Installing new coils and spark plugs is an easy task that has only two distinct points of caution. One is to make sure you do not over-tighten the spark plug into the cylinder head. Some are made of aluminum and can damage the threads in the head if they are over-tightened. The other is to make sure the coil is properly connected to the spark plug terminal to avoid any misfires and promote proper operation.

SOURCES

MSD
Autotronic Controls Corporation
1350 Pullman Drive, Dock 14
El Paso, TX 79936
(915) 857-5200
www.msdignition.com

Brisk USA Enterprises, LLC
133 N. Friendswood Dr., Suite 130
Houston, TX 77546
(713) 459-6977
www.BriskUSA.com
www.BriskRacing.com

Installing aftermarket coils and colder spark plugs is a very simple operation that can add more power at higher rpms to forced-induction engines and provide more efficient combustion for slightly improved fuel economy.

We used a set of MSD No. 84238 Blaster coils that offer improved saturation resistance by incorporating a dual-magnet design. This improves performance at higher rpms.

We also upgraded to a set of Brisk 3VR14S Silver spark plugs, which are a step colder than the factory plug and reduce the chance of detonation under boost.

The factory plug on the left, the Autolite HTO plug in the center, and the Brisk plug on the right show the different terminals. Both the factory and Autolite can't be easily gapped, a crucial factor when upgrading to colder plugs.

To remove the coil, unplug it from the harness.

A 7mm socket wrench is used to loosen and remove the retaining bolt that secures the coil to the valve cover.

Simply grab the coil from underneath and pull up. The coil should pop out from the cylinder head.

Here, you can see how the Brisk spark plug has an open terminal that's easy to gap. We gapped ours at .035 inch. Larger gaps tend to cause misfire.

To remove the factory spark plugs and install the colder plugs, you'll need a 9/16 spark plug socket. This is a specialty tool, but you can use instead a standard long socket wrench to loosen the plugs and then pull them out with a small piece of rubber fuel line hose pushed into the top terminal to grab the plug.

Carefully insert the new colder spark plug and turn it gently until it's secure to the cylinder head. Then tighten it only about a quarter turn. Be sure not to over-tighten.

ENGINE

7

Install the new coil over the spark plug by simply pushing it back into position, making sure it makes contact with the top terminal.

8

Reattach the 7mm bolt and plug the wiring harness back onto the new coil.

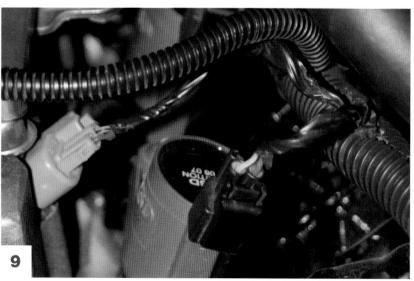

9

The process is the same for the remaining spark plugs and coils.

PROJECT 7
Adding Performance Exhaust Mufflers

A thunderous applause

Time: 30 minutes

Cost: $480

Skill level: Easy

Tools: Simple to install with standard and metric tool set, no special tools required; you will need a one-ton floor jack and jack stands

The right performance sound for your Mustang is undeniably different for many people. Some like it loud; others like it soft, deep, resonant, and so on. When choosing a performance cat-back muffler system for your Mustang, the best thing to do is listen. Pick out the system that sounds best to you by listening to other vehicles and asking the owners which muffler system they are using.

Installation is simple for a typical axle-back system and can be done in about 30 minutes if you don't have to deal with lots of dirt or rust. The results can be dramatic to your ears and really make others take notice of your Mustang.

SOURCE
Flowmaster
100 Stony Point Road, Suite 125
Santa Rosa, CA 95401
(800) 544-4761
www.flowmastermufflers.com

These Flowmaster mufflers for the 2005–2009 Mustang are from the American Thunder line of mufflers. They offer a deep tone but little interior resonance. Kit No. 17410 comes with two mufflers, clamps, and hardware, and features a black-painted finish with chromed tips.

ENGINE

1 This 2008 model was put on the dyno to get a baseline horsepower reading using the factory mufflers. On the dyno, the completely stock vehicle made 260 rear-wheel horsepower and 268 lbs-ft of torque.

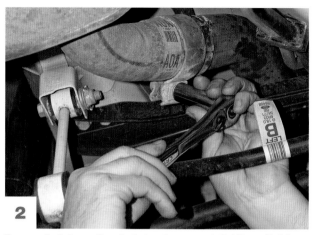

2 To remove the factory mufflers, the factory clamps are unbolted. These attach the rear of the muffler inlet to the factory exhaust pipe.

3 There are two hangars that attach to the frame. These must also be unbolted and removed. Make sure to note how they attach to the frame and twist the muffler until it comes loose from the exhaust tubing. The front hangar is removed in this photo, but you can see where it bolts onto the frame.

4 Insert the hangars onto the new mufflers and make sure the clamp is also attached. Insert the muffler over the factory pipe until it reaches the stop tab on the factory tubing. Bolt on the hangars first, then the clamp.

5 Once both sides are completed, you can enjoy the new sound. Check for leaks and tighten the clamps as necessary.

6 With the Mustang back on the dyno, we gained 5 additional horsepower and 10 lbs-ft of torque.

ENGINE

RPM	TQ base	HP base	TQ After	HP After	TQ Change	HP Change
2000	242.7	92.4	373.9	142.4	+131.2	+50.0
2100	263.8	105.5	383.2	153.2	+119.4	+47.7
2200	271.5	113.7	387.4	162.3	+115.9	+48.6
2300	273.1	119.6	396.2	173.5	+123.1	+53.9
2400	277.3	126.7	400.3	182.9	+123.0	+56.2
2500	274.0	130.4	406.8	193.6	+132.8	+63.2
2600	276.7	137.0	411.3	203.6	+134.6	+66.6
2700	281.2	144.6	415.7	213.7	+134.5	+69.1
2800	282.3	150.5	417.0	222.3	+134.7	+71.8
2900	278.4	153.7	421.7	232.9	+143.3	+79.2
3000	277.4	158.4	426.3	243.5	+148.9	+85.1
3100	276.1	163.0	429.1	253.3	+153.0	+90.3
3200	277.0	168.8	429.6	261.8	+152.6	+93.0
3300	280.9	176.5	438.6	275.6	+157.7	+99.1
3400	286.9	185.7	438.2	283.7	+151.3	+98.0
3500	293.2	195.4	441.6	294.2	+148.4	+98.8
3600	295.3	202.4	444.8	304.9	+149.5	+102.5
3700	294.4	207.4	443.6	312.5	+149.6	+105.1
3800	297.4	215.2	446.3	322.9	+148.9	+107.7
3900	300.0	222.8	448.8	333.3	+148.8	+110.5
4000	301.1	229.3	445.3	339.1	+144.3	+109.8
4100	303.3	236.8	**451.9**	352.7	+148.6	+115.9
4200	**305.7**	244.4	449.9	359.8	+144.2	+115.4
4300	304.8	249.5	446.8	365.8	+142.0	+116.3
4400	302.8	253.7	447.5	374.9	+144.7	+121.2
4500	300.6	257.6	446.3	382.4	+145.7	+124.8
4600	297.5	260.5	444.9	389.6	+147.4	+129.1
4700	296.2	265.0	444.8	398.0	+148.6	+133.0
4800	293.9	268.6	445.9	407.5	+152.0	+138.4
4900	292.4	272.8	444.0	414.2	+151.6	+141.4
5000	289.3	275.4	439.3	418.3	+150.0	+142.9
5100	286.1	**277.8**	437.3	424.6	+151.2	+146.8
5200	280.3	277.5	432.9	428.6	+152.6	+151.1
5300	274.0	276.5	432.3	436.3	+158.3	+160.3
5400	268.5	276.0	431.4	443.6	+162.9	+167.6
5500	261.1	273.4	425.3	445.4	+164.2	+172.0
5600	257.4	274.4	425.1	453.3	+167.7	+178.9
5700	253.7	275.4	422.6	458.6	+168.9	+183.2
5800	249.6	275.6	419.4	463.2	+169.8	+187.6
5900	246.3	276.7	413.5	464.6	+167.2	+187.9
6000	239.6	273.7	411.0	469.5	+171.4	+195.8
6100	235.1	273.0	407.6	473.4	+172.5	+200.4
6200	228.2	269.4	397.1	468.7	+168.9	+199.3
6300	222.1	266.4	396.9	476.1	+174.8	+209.7
6400	0	0	388.0	472.8	0	0
6500	0	0	386.8	**478.6**	0	0

ENGINE

41

PROJECT 8
Installing Custom Valve Covers

? Like a new engine

🕐 Time: 3 hours

$ Cost: $390

★ Skill level: Easy

🧰 Tools: No special tools necessary; requires SAE and metric tool set

One of the best ways to dramatically improve the look of your Mustang's engine is to upgrade to an aftermarket set of valve covers. While this may sound like an oily mess, the fact is it's very easy to do and only takes time and patience to do it correctly.

There are a wide variety of valve covers available for the 4.6-liter 3-valve engine, and they are similar in installation. Make sure your engine is completely cold when you attempt this upgrade, and you'll also have to remove the battery and battery tray on the passenger side to remove and replace the valve cover on that side. Then, make sure you use a quality valve cover. Some, like those available from Moroso, utilize factory Ford valve covers that have been powder-coated, chromed, or treated with a faux carbon-fiber look.

Once you've installed your valve covers, you'll be surprised at how much it completely transforms the appearance of your engine compartment.

SOURCE

Moroso
80 Carter Drive
Guilford, CT 06437
(203) 453-6571
www.moroso.com

ENGINE

A set of cool valve covers, like these from Moroso, can dramatically change the appearance of your engine. These are Moroso No. 68386 valve covers with a carbon-fiber design that has a clear-coat finish and all the factory components, including gasket and fasteners.

Less-expensive options are powder-coated valve covers. These are also Moroso covers (No. 68382) for the 4.6-liter 3-valve V-8.

You can get chromed or polished covers from a variety of manufacturers, but we chose the Moroso covers because of the high quality.

Some manufacturers use factory valve covers that they smooth, polish, or powder-coat. Our Moroso covers are exactly that, ensuring that the gaskets will fit and that there won't be any fitment problems on the cylinder head.

Our 4.6-liter 3-valve actually makes 500 rear-wheel horsepower, but its appearance doesn't match what's underneath the dull factory valve covers.

1

Start by completely disconnecting the wiring harness from all of the sensors.

2

Several wiring looms are also attached to the valve covers and must be released.

ENGINE

3

With the wiring loom disconnected from the fuel injectors, sensors, and coils, there's plenty of room to take out the valve cover.

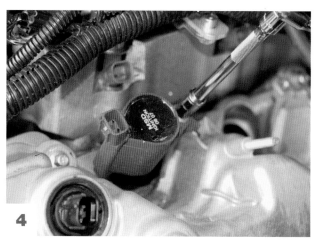

4

To remove the coils, remove the 7mm retaining bolts that hold the coil to the valve cover.

5

Using an 8mm socket wrench, loosen all of the bolts from around the valve cover. Make sure you have a couple of extensions to make it easy to reach some of the bolts.

6

With all of the bolts loose, pry out the valve cover. You may also have to remove the bolt that holds the dipstick bracket to make additional clearance. On the passenger side, you will have to remove the battery and battery tray for clearance.

7

The factory adds a dab of silicone that is left over from attaching the front case of the engine to the cylinder head. You won't have to worry about this, but make sure you clean up the cylinder head with a gasket scraper.

8

Here's what the valve and cam assembly look like with the valve cover off. We also placed rags underneath to avoid any chance of oil spilling on the exhaust.

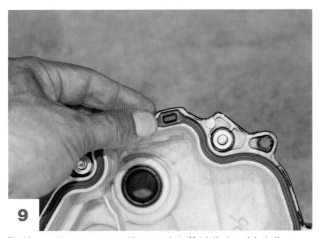

9

The Moroso valve covers come with new gaskets. Match the large tabs to the areas on the cover so that the dimples point toward you. Then push the gasket in place all around the cover.

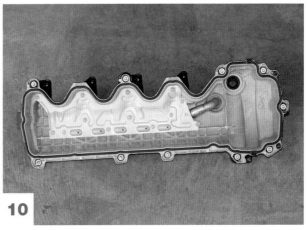

10

When done correctly, the gasket should fit around the cover perfectly.

11

The tricky part is maneuvering the valve cover around hoses and into position. It's best to be patient and slowly move the cover into place. Keep in mind you don't want to scratch the camshaft with the valve cover bolts by mistake.

12

Hand-tighten all of the valve cover bolts first. Then go back and use your wrench to tighten all of the bolts. Start in the center and work your way to the outer bolts.

13

When all the bolts are tight, reconnect your wiring harness.

14

We did the other side, and the entire process took about three hours, but it was simple to do. The end result looks awesome, and all of the factory hoses and fittings go right in place.

ENGINE

PROJECT 9
Adding a Performance Tuner and Computer System

 Get with the program

 Skill level: Easy; anyone can install

Time: 15 minutes

Tools: No tools necessary

Cost: $799

It's amazing the kind of performance you can achieve by recalibrating your Mustang's electronic control unit. Tuners reconfigure fuel curves, ignition timing, and transmission shift points and firmness that can dramatically improve performance. But aside from adding a different tune to your Mustang, some devices also work as an onboard computer to calculate horsepower and torque, feature gauge displays to monitor engine functions, and provide diagnostic input.

The Diablosport Trinity is one such device that we installed on a 2010 Mustang GT. The Trinity is a tuner and onboard computer system that places all of the vehicle's functions, monitoring, and performance tuning in one device. Like other tuners, the Trinity simply plugs into the Mustang's diagnostic port and then an easy-to-follow, touch-screen display guides you through the installation of a new vehicle tune and the unit's other functions.

Most tuners will offer performance tunes for 87-, 91-, or 93-octane fuel and have other custom tuning functions for advanced users. During the tune download, you will follow the instructions on the screen and select the appropriate application for your specific vehicle. The system will also tell you to turn the ignition key to the "on" position and then off again to reset during various stages of the installation. Once the display says that the tune is installed, you're ready to enjoy increased power and performance.

SOURCE
Diablosport
3500 N. W. Boca Raton Blvd., Suite 504
Boca Raton, FL 33431
(877) 396-6614
www.diablosport.com

Installing a performance tuner to your Mustang can yield as much as 15–20 additional horsepower and 15–20 lbs-ft of torque on 4.6-liter 3-valve GT models.

The Diablosport Trinity comes with touch-screen display on the main computer, windshield mount, diagnostic port cord, and USB computer cord to upload and save files to your home computer or laptop.

The Trinity functions and programs are available for 2005–2010 Mustang GT and GT-500 models. We opted to install one on this 2010 GT with a 4.6-liter V-8.

1

The interior of the GT doesn't leave any room for extra gauges, so we decided to use the windshield mount in this application.

2

Attach the windshield mount to the back of the Trinity by slipping it into the locking tabs.

3

The kit comes with a right-angle chord that attaches to the bottom of the unit. Route the chord along the back of the dash, under the driver's-side pillar, and up to the diagnostic port.

4

We simply plug in the chord to the diagnostic port, and the Trinity is ready for use. Just follow the instructions on the display.

5

The Trinity will monitor vital engine functions through a gauge display that is customizable.

6

On the main menu of the Trinity screen, you can go into a variety of modes, such as Performance, Diagnostics, Options, Racing, Monitoring, and Data logging.

7

Before downloading a new tune, it's always best to check if there are any existing engine trouble codes. In our application there weren't any trouble codes in the ECU.

8

The system allows you to back up the factory tune before prompting you to download one of three performance tunes for 87-, 91-, and 93-octane fuel use.

9

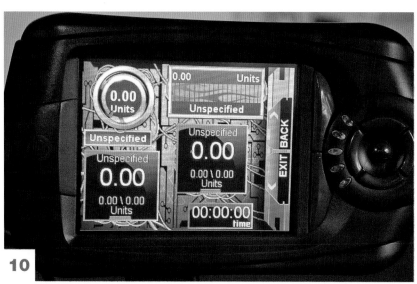

You can monitor a variety of your engine's functions by setting each gauge. You can also change the location of the gauge and the style by selecting the various options from the touch-screen menu.

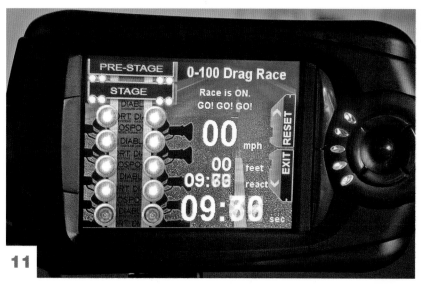

In Performance mode, the Trinity allows you to run ¼-mile, 060 mile-per-hour, and other track tests. It allows you to start from a drag racing tree or from a motion start.

You can log all your data and use the provided CD to download software that will track your data on your home computer or laptop.

PROJECT 10
Installing a Carbon-Fiber Radiator Cover

 Make your coolant system look cooler

 Time: 30 minutes

 Cost: $700 (includes fuel rail covers, radiator core cover, and plenum cover)

 Skill level: Easy; anyone can do it

 Tools: No special tools; requires flathead screwdriver and 5/16 long socket wrench and driver

When you're looking for an easy way to dramatically improve the appearance of your engine compartment, there are plenty of covers available that fit over the factory plenum and fuel rails and that replace the plastic radiator core support cover. While many are manufactured from plastic and come in a variety of colors to match your Mustang's paint scheme, we opted to go the high-end route and install a set of APR carbon-fiber units that give any engine compartment a race-inspired look your buddies will envy.

SOURCE

APR Performance Inc.
21037 Commerce Pointe Dr.
Walnut, CA 91789
(909) 594-3796
www.aprperformance.com

There's nothing like carbon fiber in an engine compartment to make your vehicle look distinctive.

ENGINE

Replacing the plastic radiator core support cover with a carbon-fiber cover is easy and will make a big impact when you open the hood.

To remove the factory cover, use a flathead screwdriver to pull up on the head of the plastic rivet, then pull the base out.

Once all six rivets are out, the plastic cover can be removed from the vehicle.

The APR carbon-fiber cover is placed into position, and the rivets are reinstalled by pushing them into place.

PROJECT 11
Installing Carbon-Fiber Fuel Rail Covers

? **A clean cover-up**

Time: 30 minutes

$ **Cost:** $195 (includes fuel rail covers, radiator core cover, and plenum cover)

★ **Skill level:** Easy; anyone can do it

Tools: No special tools; requires flathead screwdriver and ⁵⁄₁₆ long socket wrench and driver

Fuel rail covers hide the wiring and fuel rails between the plenum and valve covers.

The driver's side is the most difficult because it requires you to temporarily remove the vacuum line to the fuel rail pressure regulator, unplug the wiring harness, and remove the PCV line to the intake plenum to provide room to set in the cover.

ENGINE

It's also a good idea to move the rear wiring loom from the firewall for extra slack, providing more room to insert the fuel rail cover.

2

Slide the cover into position under the fuel return line, making sure the holes line up and fit over the existing fuel rail studs. The wiring loom tabs will fit over the covers and hold them in place.

3

Here's what it looks like once all the hoses and the wiring harness are reattached. The passenger side has no hoses to interfere with the installation, so it is easier to put in.

4

ENGINE

PROJECT 12
Installing Carbon-Fiber Plenum Cover

 Is your intake plenum naked? Cover it up!

 Skill level: Easy; anyone can do it

 Time: 30 minutes

Tools: No special tools; requires flathead screwdriver and ⁵⁄₁₆ long socket wrench and driver

Cost: $185 (includes fuel rail covers, radiator core cover, and plenum cover)

If your Mustang didn't come with the optional Pony plenum cover, this carbon-fiber cover from APR actually looks even better than the plastic factory unit.

1 With the fuel rail cover already installed, you simply place the plenum cover over the fuel rail studs and then secure it with the wiring loom tabs that also fit over the studs.

2 Reinsert the fuel rail studs, and the installation is completed. The plenum cover should clear a strut tower brace, but check the clearance beforehand to be sure. These pieces are vacuum formed and feature a heat-resistant epoxy coating, so they won't fade and will have a high-gloss finish for a long time.

ENGINE

55

PROJECT 13
Installing a Billet Engine Cap Kit

? **Capping it all off**

Time: 15 minutes

$ **Cost:** $200–$325, depending on product

★ **Skill level:** Easy; can be done by beginner or novice

Tools: No special tools; 3/16 Allen wrench and 3/32 or smaller punch

Billet dress-up components for your Mustang's engine compartment are easy to find and can help make your engine compartment look impressive. For example, you can replace some of the fluid caps in your Mustang's engine compartment with a set of brushed billet caps that are precision-machined and look great.

For this project, we used a Shelby Performance Engine Cap Kit (No. 7S3Z-GT-CAPS) made from 6061 billet aluminum on a 4.6-liter V-8. This is the same set of caps available exclusively on Shelby GT vehicles. The set replaces the oil, radiator, washer fluid, power steering, and brake reservoir plastic factory caps, as well as the original yellow dipstick handle.

SOURCE

Shelby Performance Parts LLC
130 Cassia Way
Henderson, NV 89014
(702) 405-3500
www.shelbyperformanceparts.com

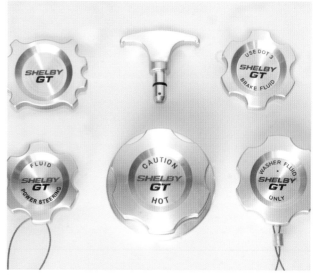

Replacing your factory engine fluid caps with billet caps is a quick and easy way to add flair to your engine compartment.

You might think a GT with a supercharger is cool enough, but we decided to use Shelby Performance Engine Cap Kit No. 7S3Z-GT-CAPS to replace the factory caps and oil dipstick handle as shown here, to enhance the engine a bit more.

1

ENGINE

Most of the caps can replace the factory plastic units. Some have a retaining strap that is simply removed by pulling it over the stud.

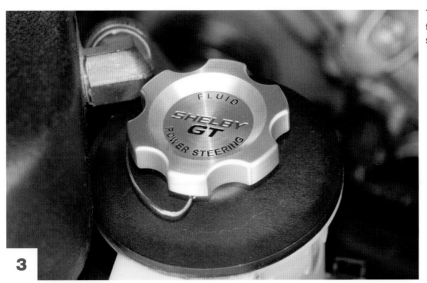

This billet cap features a wire retaining strap that fits over the factory stud. The cap simply twists into place. The same is done for the window washer fluid cap.

In this instance, the Shelby Performance billet radiator cap cover uses an adhesive. Peel away the adhesive cover and place the cap over the factory unit.

Because the radiator cap gets hot, Shelby Performance added an Allen screw to secure the cap in place. Use a ³⁄₁₆ Allen wrench to tighten the bolt.

5

Remove the factory brake fluid reservoir cap and cover the reservoir with a clean cloth to avoid excessive contact with the air. Then simply pull out the rubber liner in the cap and place it into the Shelby Performance billet unit.

6

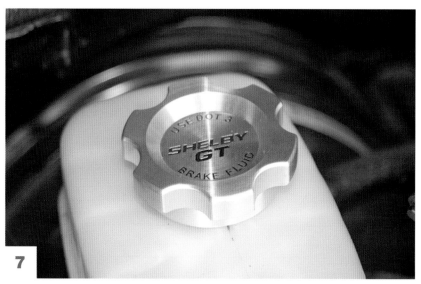

Once installed, the brake fluid reservoir looks great, and the CNC machining ensures an airtight fit.

7

ENGINE

The engine oil cap is easily removed and replaced from the passenger side valve cover. On this supercharged motor, the cap is hidden under the air intake tube. On non-supercharged models, the cap will be at the end of a plastic extension tube.

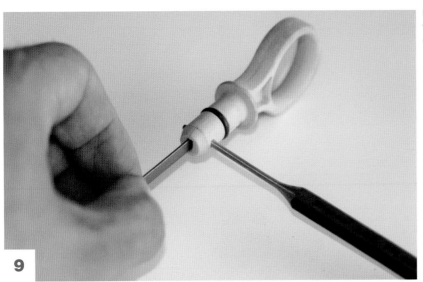

Using a small ³⁄₃₂ punch you can remove the pin securing the dipstick handle to the dipstick. Be sure to avoid damaging the handle or dipstick if you're using a vice.

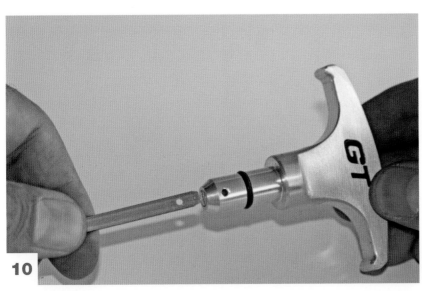

Once the factory handle is removed, the dipstick fits into the Shelby T-handle. Check to make sure the dipstick goes on correctly. The handle should have the GT logo facing away from the engine.

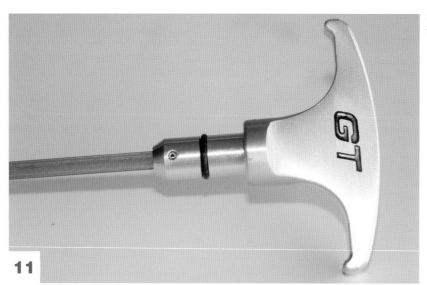

Using a small hammer, tap in the retaining pin to secure the factory dipstick to the Shelby T-handle.

11

Here's what it looks like when it's installed back into the engine.

12

With only a few new billet details, your engine can look much more impressive.

13

SECTION 2
SUSPENSION

PROJECT 14
Lowering the Front End

 Lowering with performance coils and shocks

 Time: 3 hours

$ **Cost:** Shocks, $550; coil spring set, $230

 Skill level: Moderate to difficult; requires experience in removing and reinstalling suspension components in the correct order and placement

 Tools: Spring compressor required for front spring replacement; this can be done with a hydraulic floor jack and jack stands, but access to a lift makes installation much easier

Once your cornering speeds increase, you begin to notice that the factory suspension tends to roll, flex, and pitch in a way that makes you feel uneasy. That's the time to upgrade to a set of performance shocks and coil springs. As an added benefit, this type of upgrade also lowers your vehicle from 1.3–1.5 inches, depending on the coil spring manufacturer. There are many shock and spring manufacturers to choose from, but this is an upgrade that you only want to do once. So it pays to get the highest-quality components available to prevent spring sag and shock absorber failure over time.

We selected a set of Vogtland coil springs that lower the Mustang 1.3 inches in the front and rear. These springs feature a 10-year guarantee against sagging and are among the highest-quality springs available due to the type of metal used. To complement the springs, we also elected to use the Tokico D-Spec adjustable shocks. These are very popular because they can be tuned for the street or racecourse with an adjustable knob that's easily accessible at the top of the shock.

The combination of these springs and shocks lowered our Mustang GT about 1 inch in front and 1.5 inches in the rear. But more importantly, the car's handling was dramatically improved, keeping the Mustang flat on tight turns at speed. The adjustable Tokico shocks allowed us to tune in the dampening, hard for the road course and soft for the street. A good compromise was three turns in, providing for excellent street performance without a harsh ride.

While the installation is simple, you will need access to a spring compressor to properly remove the front springs from the struts. This is mandatory to avoid the possibility of injury. Most alignment shops will have one and will charge you about $10–$20 per spring, making your installation much easier.

SOURCES

Vogtland North America
43391 Business Park Dr., Suite C10
Temecula, CA 92590
(951) 694-6981
www.vogtland-na.com

Tokico
475 Alaska Ave
Torrance, CA 90503
(310) 212-0200
www.tokicogasshocks.com

Shelby Performance Parts
130 Cassia Way
Henderson, NV 89014
(702) 405-3500
www.shelbyperformanceparts.com

Install:
Pure Motorsport
41740 Enterprise Circle N., Suite 108
Temecula, CA 92590
(866) 397-5487
www.purems.com

This is what our Mustang looked like before we lowered it. Notice the extra space between the wheelwells and our set of 20-inch Shelby Razor wheels and Toyo Proxes 4 tires.

Upgrading to performance coil springs and shocks is a great way to improve handling and to lower the ride height of your Mustang GT. This is what ours looked like after the springs and shocks were installed.

1

The guys from Pure Motorsport helped us with the installation and measured the vehicle's height from the centerline of the wheel to the lip of the wheelwell.

2

After the vehicle was secured on a lift, they began by unbolting the top shock mount bolts on the strut tower.

3

With the wheels removed from the vehicle, the two lower shock mounts are unbolted from the spindle.

4

Remove the clip that connects the brake line to the strut, and then the entire strut assembly is removed.

5 The strut assembly removed. You can see that the top shock nut holds the spring perch in place and must be unbolted.

6 It's very important to use a proper spring compressor tool. An alignment shop will have one, and they will charge you a nominal fee to compress the spring for you.

7 With the spring safely compressed, you can unbolt the top bolt.

8 Here you can see the height difference between the factory spring on the right and the Vogtland spring on the left.

9 Check the top spring perch to make sure there's no damage to the ball bearings. If it's excessively worn, you'll hear a popping noise every time it compresses.

10 The Tokico D-Spec shocks are a great upgrade over the factory units. They can be adjusted to multiple positions and have been shown to work great on the street and track.

11

The coil spring must sit properly in the spring perch before it is reinstalled. Note how the rubber isolator is notched to accommodate the spring.

12

Using the compressor, the new spring is installed on the strut assembly.

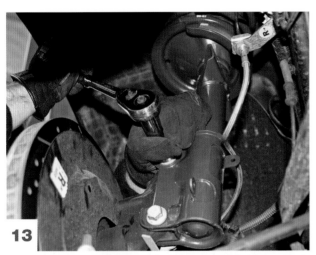

13

After installing the top first through the holes in the strut tower, the lower portion of the strut assembly is bolted onto the spindle.

14

The sway bar end links are also reattached to the brackets on the Tokico strut.

15

Here's what the assembly looks like once it's been bolted back into position.

PROJECT 15
Lowering the Rear

 Lowering the rear suspension with springs and shocks

 Time: 3 hours

$ Cost: Shocks, $550; coil spring set, $230

 Skill level: Moderate to difficult; requires experience in removing and reinstalling suspension components in the correct order and placement

 Tools: This can be done with a hydraulic floor jack and jack stands, but access to a lift makes installation much easier

SOURCES

Vogtland North America
43391 Business Park Dr., Suite C10
Temecula, CA 92590
(951) 694-6981
www.vogtland-na.com

Tokico
475 Alaska Ave
Torrance, CA 90503
(310) 212-0200
www.tokicogasshocks.com

Shelby Performance Parts
130 Cassia Way
Henderson, NV 89014
(702) 405-3500
www.shelbyperformanceparts.com

Install:
Pure Motorsport
41740 Enterprise Circle N., Suite 108
Temecula, CA 92590
(866) 397-5487
www.purems.com

1 You should also be sure to let the rear drop, allowing you more room to remove the rear coils.

2 Removing the bottom bolts on the rear shocks will allow the rear axle to drop down even farther. You should use a jack stand or support to avoid letting it come down too far.

SUSPENSION

3

The top of the rear sway bar end link is also unbolted to allow the axle to drop down farther.

4

With the axle moved down, the pressure is removed from the rear coils, and they can be removed from the spring perch.

5

The Vogtland coils are simply put back into the factory spring perches. You should also make sure that the rubber isolators are removed from the factory springs and replaced onto the new springs.

6

The rear shocks are still held in place from the top mounts, which can be accessed from inside the trunk.

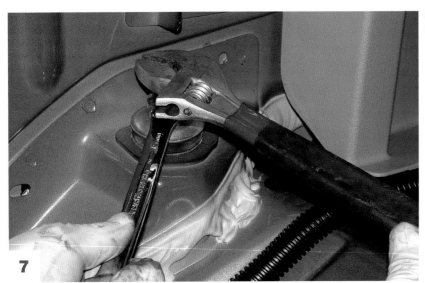

An adjustable wrench holds the top of the shock while you unbolt the nut holding it in place.

Attach the bottom of the rear shock to the axle using the factory hardware.

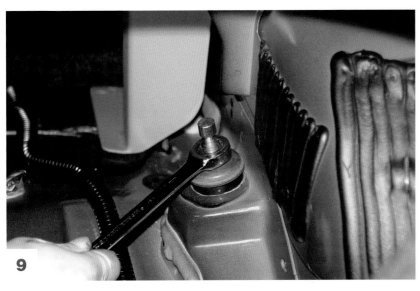

The top of the new shock is installed through the trunk. The top bolt is tightened until the bushing begins to deform under pressure.

Once both shocks are in place, a jack stand is used to push the axle back up so that you can reattach the sway bar end links and ensure that the top of the shocks are secured properly.

A small hacksaw is used to trim off the top section of the bump stop, giving you additional axle articulation for the lowered ride height.

In this application, we installed a set of 20×9-inch Shelby Razor wheels from Shelby Performance and mounted them to a set of Toyo Proxes 4 tires. This extra tire width should also dramatically improve our Mustang's handling abilities and improve its appearance.

PROJECT 16
Adding a Performance Anti-Sway Bar

 Improving your Mustang's handling

 Time: 2 hours

Cost: Front anti-sway bar, $245

 Skill level: Easy; simple to install with standard and metric tool set

 Tools: No special tools required; use of lift makes this job much easier, but it can be done with four jack stands and a heavy-duty floor jack

The function the anti-sway bar plays in your Mustang's suspension system is often overlooked. Performance front and rear anti-sway bars differ from the factory units in their size and density. This difference results in less resistance to body roll, which can limit the weight transfer of the body over the tires. Keeping the vehicle's weight as neutral as possible over all four tires during hard cornering greatly improves traction, and you move faster in the turns.

Replacing the factory 34mm front and 20mm rear anti-sway bars is an easy task that will yield some excellent results. Some anti-sway bars like those we installed from Whiteline Automotive are adjustable to increase the bar's stiffness; a great option if you plan on taking your Mustang on an autocross or to the road track.

SOURCES

Whiteline Automotive
Global Performance Parts
4554 128th Ave.
Holland, MI 49424
(616) 399-9025
www.GlobalPerformanceParts.com

Install:
J. Bittle American Performance Center
5135 Convoy St.
San Diego, CA 92111
(848) 495-3395

SUSPENSION

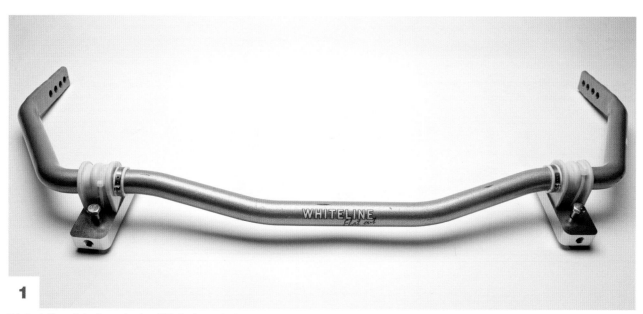

1

This front aftermarket anti-sway bar from Whiteline Automotive is 32mm, 2mm smaller than the factory anti-sway bar. The Whiteline bar is different because it is solid, as opposed to the hollow factory bar. The solid bar allows for more resistance to body roll, and with the extra four holes at the ends, the Whiteline anti-sway bar can be adjusted for the track.

Weak points on both the GT and GT-500 Mustang's suspensions are the mounting points for the front anti-sway bars. These have been known to break and twist under hard cornering. You should remove the factory brackets from their location on the radiator core support.

The factory anti-sway bar is also unbolted from the lower portion of the sway-bar end links on both sides of the vehicle.

Once everything is unbolted, the factory anti-sway bar can be removed from the vehicle.

5 The Whiteline anti-sway bar uses new urethane bushings and an aluminum block that strengthens the mounting point of the center bushings. A new bracket and retaining plate fit behind the block.

6 We set the Whiteline anti-sway bar on the stock setting for the end links. The holes add a 14 percent, 32 percent, and 53 percent increase in stiffness over stock. We recommend using these settings, with the help of an experienced race suspension expert, if you plan on taking your Mustang to the track.

PROJECT 17
Adding a Rear Performance Anti-Sway Bar

 Minimize understeer with a larger rear anti-sway bar

 Time: 2 hours

 Cost: Rear anti-sway bar, $200

 Skill level: Easy; simple to install with standard and metric tool set

 Tools: No special tools required; use of lift makes this job much easier, but it can be done with four jack stands and a heavy-duty floor jack

SOURCES

Whiteline Automotive
Global Performance Parts
4554 128th Ave.
Holland, MI 49424
(616) 399-9025
www.GlobalPerformanceParts.com

Install:
J. Bittle American Performance Center
5135 Convoy St.
San Diego, CA 92111
(848) 495-3395

If your Mustang came with a rear anti-sway bar, it measures 20mm and was designed to reduce the vehicle's tendency for understeer. In this application, we used a Whiteline rear anti-sway bar that measures 26mm in diameter.

Removing the factory rear anti-sway bar begins with unbolting the mounting brackets.

Then the top portion of the anti-sway bar end links are unbolted on both sides.

The factory rear anti-sway bar is then removed from the chassis.

Because the Whiteline anti-sway bar is larger, it requires removing the sway bar and the factory bushings from the end links and replacing them with the Whiteline urethane units.

The end links for the new bushings are slipped onto the Whiteline bar and can then be reinstalled into the chassis.

New bushings are also added to the sway bar's mounting points, but the factory brackets are still used.

This Mustang is now set to take on corners at high speeds. During our initial tests, the body remained incredibly flat, and the rubber on the tires was the only limiting factor on how fast we could take a corner.

PROJECT 18
Installing an Adjustable Panhard Rod

 Adjust your rear

 Skill level: Medium

Time: 1 hour

 Tools: Must have access to a lift and axle stands to support the axle

Cost: Panhard rod, $195; Panhard rod support, $110; Panhard rod bracket, $73

The S197 Mustang's rear suspension uses an upper and two lower control arms that center the axle and control the pinion angle. It's the job of the Panhard rod to keep the axle from moving side to side. While the factory Panhard rod setup works fine under normal driving conditions, it tends to flex and distort when cornering at higher speeds. Furthermore, if your Mustang is lowered, the weight transfer under cornering will be even greater and will cause the factory Panhard rod unit to flex.

While this isn't necessarily a major problem for some, it does cause great concern if you are planning on using the widest tires you can stuff into your Mustang's rear wheelwells. Limiting side-to-side movement and being able to properly adjust the body over the axle is crucial when you are using a tire that has a much wider section width than stock, such as a P275, 285, or 305.

Our installation was done at J Bittle American Performance Center in San Diego, California, where we found that installing an aftermarket Panhard rod is easy. The only requirement is that the vehicle be at stock ride height when you install it to avoid any preload on the bearings that might cause premature wear.

JBA installed a BMR adjustable Panhard rod (No. MPHR012) on a 2007 Mustang GT. The rod features spherical rod ends and is made from 1.25 DOM steel tubing, making it a heavy-duty piece for this aggressive car. This Panhard rod allows for easy on-car adjustability at the track, and when used with a stronger upper Panhard rod support, it will ensure that the rear won't move at all from side to side. We also used the BMR Panhard rod bracket that moves the Panhard rod mounting point on the axle 1 inch farther away from the differential cover. This will allow extra clearance to run an aftermarket aluminum differential cover.

SOURCES

BMR Fabrication
12581 US Highway 301 N
Thonotosassa, FL 33592
(813) 986-9302
www.bmrfabrication.com

J Bittle American Performance Center
5135 Convoy St.
San Diego, CA 92111
(888) 522-5570
www.jbaracing.com

Upgrading the Panhard rod and upper bracket (shown in red) is a sure way to control the side-to-side axle movement on your Mustang.

SUSPENSION

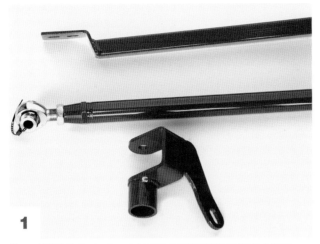

1 We used BMR's Panhard rod, upper bracket, and relocation bracket on a street Mustang that is also driven on a road coarse during weekend races. The advantages are increased strength and being able to make adjustments at the track.

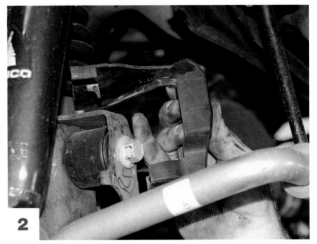

2 A plastic cover is removed to access the Panhard rod bolt that attaches to the axle.

3 Begin unbolting the Panhard rod by first removing the bolt on the chassis.

4 Then remove the bolt from the Panhard's axle mount so that the rod can be taken away from the vehicle.

5 The upper mount is then unbolted from the chassis mount.

6 Remove the two bolts on the Mustang's frame.

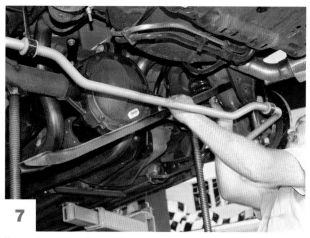

7 You may have to use a large pry bar to remove the top bar bolt because it is a close fit between the mount and the coil spring.

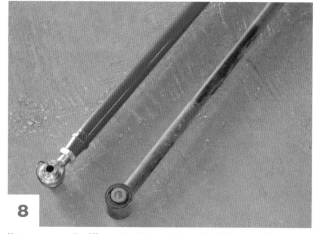

8 Here you can see the difference in thickness between the BMR rod and the factory rod. The spherical bearing on the BMR rod will also eliminate flex and provide precise control of the rear axle. We also adjusted the rod so that it was the same length as the stock unit.

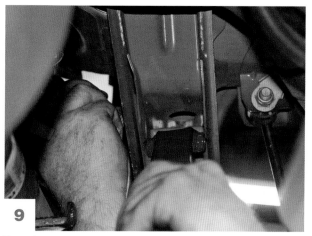

9 The top bar goes in using the factory bolt.

10 The factory bolts also secure the top bar to the Mustang's frame.

11 The Panhard rod relocation bracket attaches to the bottom shock mount bolt. Remove the anti-sway bar mounts to move the sway bar back and have access to the bolt.

12 With the anti-sway bar out of the way, you can remove the driver's-side shock mount bolt.

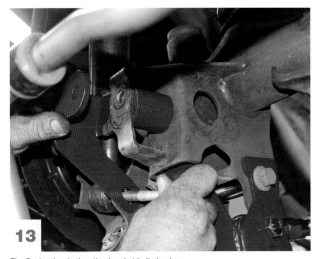

13 The Panhard rod relocation bracket bolts in place.

14 New hardware is provided to bolt the Panhard rod through the new mount.

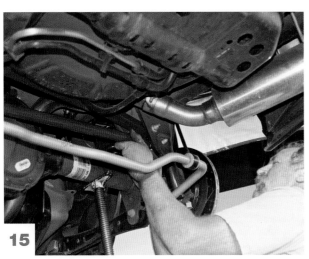

15 The other end of the Panhard rod is bolted to the chassis.

16 Once in place, everything is tightened up, and the anti-sway bar mounts are reinstalled.

17 The finished installation looks great and will give this Mustang improved cornering with the ability to make quick adjustments.

PROJECT 19
Installing Front Chassis Bracing

 A supporting role

 Time: 2 hours

Cost: Front chassis brace, $220; control arm brace, $150

 Skill level: Easy

 Tools: Simple to install with standard and metric tool set; no special tools required

While some Mustang owners like to install a strut tower brace to help minimize chassis flex, most of the movement that happens under hard cornering is actually under the vehicle. Various tests have shown that under hard cornering, chassis flex can account for as much as one degree variance in static alignment settings. On the S197 Mustangs, the factory realized this and added a control arm brace crossmember on convertible models to eliminate extra flex in this area.

Because the Mustang's suspension extends from the anti-sway bar's mounting points on the radiator core support at the front to the crossmember where the front control arms are located, it makes sense to connect this area with added bracing. We installed a Whiteline Automotive front chassis brace and rear control arm brace and noticed a dramatic improvement in steering response and sensitivity. The braces

are also lightweight and use factory holes in the chassis to mount in place without drilling.

SOURCES

Whiteline Automotive
Global Performance Parts
4554 128th Ave.
Holland, MI 49424
(616) 399-9025
www.GlobalPerformanceParts.com

Install:
JBA Performance Center
5135 Convoy St.
San Diego, CA 92111
(888) 522-5570
www.jbaracing.com

Under hard cornering, stresses can flex the factory chassis to a point where there are significant changes in the vehicle's alignment settings.

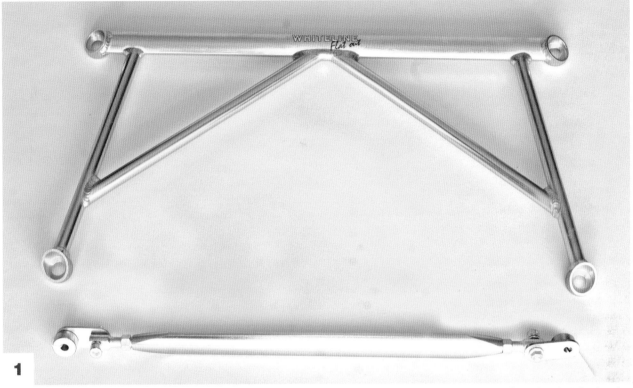

1

These chassis braces offer better suspension support when compared to strut tower braces. For supercharged cars that can't fit a strut tower brace, these front chassis and control arm braces from Whiteline Automotive are a must.

2

The control arm braces simply bolt onto the factory location on the control arms. A similar brace is used on convertible models to minimize flex. These braces use heavy-duty hardware and are adjustable.

3 Once installed, it's easy to see how the braces can add support to the chassis in this area.

4 Under hard cornering, there's lot of stress placed on the front anti-sway bar mounts indicated here. It also increases pressure against the bottom of the radiator core support.

5 Attaching the chassis brace that connects this area with the crossmember begins by unbolting the anti-sway bar mounts.

6 Aluminum spacers mount the anti-sway bar back a bit and provide a mounting point for the front bolts on the brace. The rear brace is mounted to a pair of factory holes in the crossmember.

7

Here you can see how the front anti-sway bar is mounted and how the brace bolts to the bottom of the spacers.

8

At the rear of the brace, Nylock bolts are slipped into the crossmember, allowing the bolts to secure the rear in place.

9 The aluminum front brace fits close to the front rack-and-pinion unit, but it doesn't touch.

10 With the crossmember and radiator core support connected, our steering response and feel improved dramatically. It was surprising to realize how much movement was taking place before we added these support pieces.

PROJECT 20
Installing a Front Suspension Anti-Dive Kit

 No diving allowed

 Time: 4 hours

 Cost: $340 (product)

 Skill level: Moderate; can be done by a novice

 Tools: No special tools; requires access to a press and a small-diameter press plate that fits around the control arm bushing shaft

It's embarrassing when your Mustang's front end dives down and the rear comes up when you step on the brakes. The S197 Mustang's tendency to nose-dive is due to the big, soft, rubber bushings located on the vehicle's front lower control arms. Under braking, the bushing can't absorb all of the vehicle's weight that shifts forward, so it has a tendency to flex. The result is that it allows the center of gravity to move over the vehicle and push down on the front end.

There are bushings available that replace the factory units, but some of them simply stuff a urethane donut into the factory housing or replace the entire unit with a heavy-duty urethane bushing and housing that is designed more for racing applications. Whiteline Suspension makes an anti-dive kit that is more compliant than race-style bushing replacements, yet it is firmer than the factory bushing. This unit completely replaces the factory bushing and has a built-in camber adjustment that improves steering response. This two-point static caster adjustment (up to 0.75 degrees) allows you to exit out of corners faster, which can improve your lap times at autocrosses or on a road course.

On the street and highway, we noticed a dramatic reduction in the vehicle's nose-dive tendencies under moderate to hard braking. We then took the Mustang on a short road course where we noticed a slight improvement in steering response when turning into corners. Exiting corners at higher speeds, however, we found the caster adjustment made it much easier and quicker to unwind the steering wheel and accelerate out of the corner. We also didn't experience any road noise or uncomfortable vibration from this bushing replacement.

SOURCES

Whiteline Automotive
Global Performance Parts
4554 128th Ave.
Holland, MI 49424
(616) 399-9025
www.GlobalPerformanceParts.com

Install:
JBA Performance Center
5135 Convoy St.
San Diego, CA 92111
(888) 522-5570
www.jbaracing.com

The large control arm bushing flexes and allows the weight to transfer over the top of the vehicle, instead of through the frame.

A simple urethane bushing upgrade, such as this one from Whiteline Automotive, will cure the problem. It can also add improved steering response and doesn't affect the ride quality of the vehicle.

SUSPENSION

1

The first step in changing the bushings is to unbolt the control arm from the factory spindle.

2

The front control arm bushing bolt is easy to reach, but the rack-and-pinion steering unit is in the way of removing the bolt from the frame.

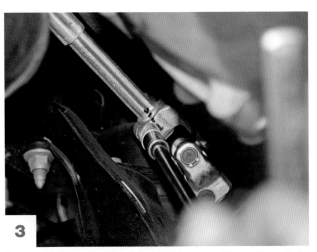

3

The rack-and-pinion unit will have to be unbolted and moved forward slightly. To do this, you first need to loosen the steering shaft U-joint.

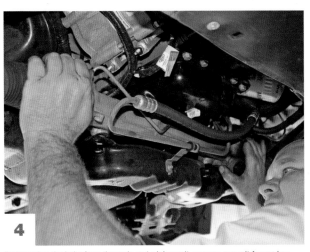

4

By removing the bolts from the rack-and-pinion unit, you can move it forward an inch or two.

5

With the rack-and-pinion unit moved forward, you can remove the front control arm bolt.

6

At the rear of the control arm, you simply remove the two bolts that secure the bushing housing to the frame.

7 Once everything is loose, you can remove the control arm.

8 Check to make sure the front bushing and the ball joint are in good condition.

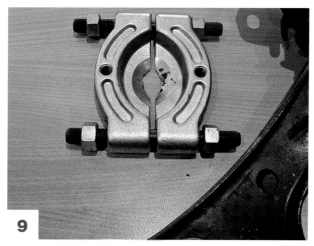

9 To remove the factory bushing, you'll need a press and a puller like this to ensure you get a grip on the inner bushing sleeve.

10 The press will allow you to remove the bushing in one piece, but make sure the puller or press plates are secure on the inner sleeve. Otherwise you'll end up with the bushing fluid all over the place.

11 Here's what the control arm spigot looks like without the factory bushing. The Whiteline anti-dive kit comes with a new sleeve that fits over the spigot.

12 Carefully position the sleeve over the spigot and use a press to push it into place.

13

With a dab of silicone grease, the Whiteline bushing is inserted over the sleeve, and the control arm is ready to be reinstalled.

14

Reinsert the front control arm bushing bolts and spindle bolt, and reposition the rack-and-pinion unit before tightening them all up.

15

The rear control arm bushings have offset washers. Follow the instructions to place the washers in a neutral position or with increased caster for improved steering response.

16

The finished installation is time consuming but simple. For 2005-model Mustangs that have heat shields over the factory bushing, the anti-dive kit has brackets to accommodate these as well.

On the track, the Mustang comes out of the corners much quicker, allowing you to unwind the steering wheel faster. On the street, the nose-dive tendency is dramatically reduced, and this upgrade is a great start to improving your Mustang's handling abilities.

17

PROJECT 21
Installing a Strut Tower Brace

 Strut your stuff

 Time: 15 minutes

$ **Cost:** $59–$320, depending on style and manufacturer

 Skill level: Easy; bolts on with no modifications or necessary experience

 Tools: Standard and metric long socket wrench set, adjustable wrench, box end wrench set

When race teams first started bracing the two strut towers on the early 1965 Mustangs, it quickly became normal practice for performance street enthusiasts to do the same. At the time, the sheet metal around the struts was weak, especially when taking corners at high speeds around a racecourse. Modern S197-model Mustangs have a stronger chassis that doesn't necessarily need this extra support, but the extra rigidity couldn't hurt.

There are many strut tower braces available that range from a simple single tube as found on the factory Shelby GT-500 models to race-style dual braces that are fully adjustable and offer superior support. Likewise they range in price, starting around $60 for a simple chromed piece to more than $300 for braces that use billet adaptor plates and heim joints. Take note that some strut tower braces will not fit over the factory plenum cover or over an aftermarket supercharger. Be sure to ask the manufacturer which brace works best with your application.

SOURCE

Granatelli Motorsports
1000 Yarnell Place
Oxnard, CA 93033
(804) 466-6644
www.granatellimotorsports.com

SUSPENSION

This Granatelli Motorsports race-style brace features billet end caps, heim-joint rod ends, and dual adjustable, stainless-steel braces. It's on the higher end of the price scale but gives a serious look to your engine compartment while providing added stiffness for improved cornering.

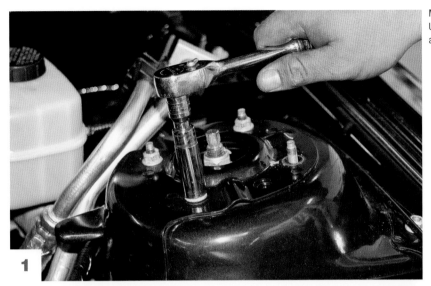

Most braces simply bolt on under the factory strut studs. Unbolt the nuts from the strut tower and do only one side at a time.

Place the billet brace plate over the studs and reinstall the factory bolts.

Install the opposite billet brace, then the dual strut rods using the supplied hardware.

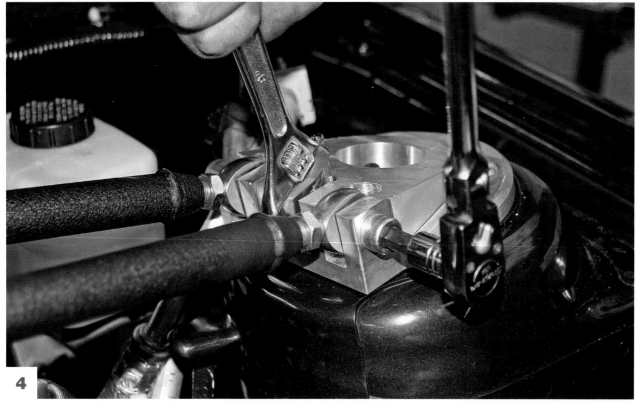

4 Make sure the rod-end bolts are tight on the billet brace plate. Tighten all four ends on this dual rod brace.

5 Once both sides are done, you've improved the look and the handling characteristics of your Mustang.

PROJECT 22
Adding an Adjustable Upper Control Arm

 Keeping your rear in control

 Time: 2 hours

Cost: $180

Skill level: Medium

Tools: Must have access to a lift, pinion angle finder, Torx-head socket wrench set, lube gun, and extra axle jacks to support the fuel tank

The Mustang's solid rear axle suspension is a proven performer. But it has its weak points. While most enthusiasts upgrade the two lower control arms to prevent wheel hop, many leave the upper control arm in stock condition. The upper control arm keeps the axle straight and maintains the pinion angle for optimal launch and traction capabilities.

An adjustable upper control arm can not only give you an advantage of added strength in this area, but it can also allow you to set your pinion angle for optimum traction and acceleration out of a turn, or for hard launches off the drag strip. Upgrading the upper control arm is easy if you have all the right tools. The most important is an angle finder that will allow you to measure the pinion angle with the vehicle in its static position.

Automatic transmission cars can improve with an angle of 1–2 degrees negative, while manual cars can be adjusted to 2–3 degrees negative as a starting point. If you're not sure, always set the angle to zero to begin.

SOURCES

BMR Fabrication
12581 US Highway 301 N
Thonotosassa, FL 33592
(813) 986-9302
www.bmrfabrication.com

Install:
J. Bittle American Performance Center
5135 Convoy St.
San Diego, CA 92111
(888) 522-5570
www.jbaracing.com

SUSPENSION

The upper control arm is the center point of your Mustang's rear suspension system. Adding a stronger, adjustable arm will provide improved traction and handling.

93

It's important to measure the factory pinion angle. The car must be at its static ride height. We used a straight edge on the pinion and measured the angle with an angle finder, which indicated it was at zero degrees.

While the vehicle is on the ground, remove the back seat by pushing the cushions in from the edge and pulling the seat out.

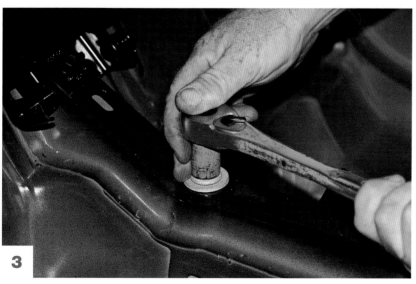

The big bolt in the center is what holds the upper control arm front mount. It must be removed first and will be difficult to break loose.

Because the front mount sits in the body with a pin, there's no way to remove it without dropping the fuel tank. With the vehicle on a lift, support the tank with a block of wood and an axle stand.

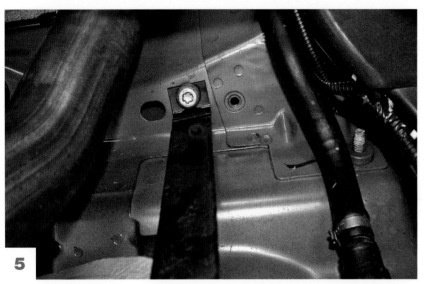

A Torx-head bolt is loosened to remove the straps on both sides of the tank. Then you can carefully lower the tank a few inches.

Unbolt the two remaining bolts that secure the upper control arm mount to the chassis, as well as the bolt that attaches the rear of the control arm to the differential housing.

Here, you can see the factory upper control arm mount and arm removed.

On a vice, unbolt the front bushing of the control arm from the mount.

Here, you can see the comparison of the BMR adjustable arm on the left with the factory arm on the right. The BMR unit is made from ⅝-inch, 0.12 wall DOM steel tubing with MIG welds. It's much stronger than the stamped-steel factory unit.

The BMR upper control arm is adjusted to the exact length of the factory arm.

Using the factory hardware, the BMR arm is attached to the factory mount.

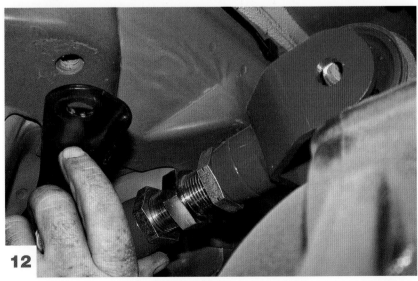

With the gas tank still lowered, the new arm and mount are reinserted into position.

13

The two mount bolts and differential mount bushing bolt are reinstalled.

14

All of the bolts are torqued to 129 lbs-ft according to the instructions.

15

The urethane bushing on the BMR adjustable upper control arm has a Zerk fitting, allowing it to be lubricated.

16

Once everything is tightened and the fuel tank is put back into place, make sure the Mustang is at a static height and re-measure the pinion angle. Our angle was zero degrees, and on this five-speed model, we could add 2–3 degrees negative to improve our traction on the drag strip.

PROJECT 23
Adding Rear Lower Control Arms

 Got it under control

 Time: 2 hours

$ **Cost:** Control arms, $260; relocation brackets, $135

 Skill level: Medium

 Tools: Must have access to a lift or jack stands to support the axle

Spinning your tires is great for show, but it doesn't do much for winning races. If you're serious about getting more traction from your modified S197 Mustang, then you can take steps to improve stiffness, limit flex, and make easy adjustments for various applications.

Wheel hop and loss of traction under acceleration is due to the flex in the Mustang's stamped-steel control arms and soft rubber bushings. An aftermarket set of rear control arms will eliminate any unwanted flex and use the vehicle's inertia to push down on the rear axle, thus improving traction.

Most aftermarket rear control arms will be made from tube steel or billet aluminum and will be outfitted with polyurethane bushings. While nonadjustable rear control arms will do wonders to improve traction on your Mustang, a set of adjustable arms will allow you to easily and quickly set up the rear suspension for drag racing or road race applications.

We decided to use an adjustable set of arms from BMR that feature a polyurethane bushing on the chassis end and a heavy-duty spherical bushing on the suspension end. This gives us the best of both street and racing control arms with full adjustability. We also installed a set of BMR's control arm relocation brackets, since they allow for proper setting of the vehicle's "instant center," which determines the amount of weight transfer to the rear axle. They also give us two levels of adjustment for street and racing use, as opposed to the factory control arm mounts.

SOURCES

BMR Fabrication
12581 US Highway 301 N
Thonotosassa, FL 33592
(813) 986-9302
www.bmrfabrication.com

J Bittle American Performance Center
5135 Convoy St.
San Diego, CA 92111
(888) 522-5570
www.jbaracing.com

SUSPENSION

The BMR rear control arms (No. TCA-201) allow us to make adjustments and are strong enough to handle this Mustang's 500 rear-wheel horsepower.

The factory stamped-steel control arms can flex under hard cornering, and the rubber bushings distort under hard acceleration. This causes wheel hop and loss of traction.

1

We had J Bittle American Performance Center in San Diego, California, install the arms for us. They began by raising the Mustang onto a lift and unbolting the rear control arm bolts. If you don't have access to a drive-on lift, you'll have to use axle stands to provide preload to the rear axle that keeps it at the vehicle's normal ride height.

2

The parking brake cable must be removed from the brake. Pull up on the cable, then remove the retaining clip, and the cable detaches from the brake caliper.

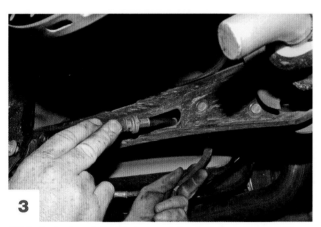

3

With the front and rear bolts of the lower control arm loose, you can unthread the cable out from the center of the factory arm.

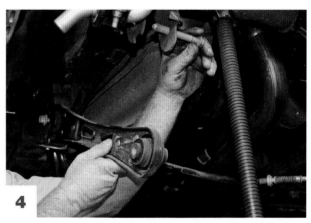

4

Once the parking brake cable is out, you can remove the front and rear bolts of the control arm to take it away from the chassis.

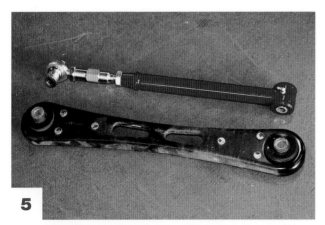

5

Here you can see the large rubber bushings on the factory control arm. The BMR arm is made from chrome-moly steel and won't flex under hard acceleration or cornering.

6

Race-style control arms use stronger spherical rod ends, while street versions use polyurethane bushings. These BMR units feature polyurethane ends that attach to the chassis and high-quality spherical rod ends on the suspension side. This provides race-style strength with little or no noise or vibrations felt by the driver when used on the street.

7 Before you install the BMR control arms, they must be adjusted to be the same length as the factory arms.

8 The polyurethane bushing end attaches to the Mustang's chassis. Note the grease fitting that adds lubrication to prevent squeaks and allows for proper movement.

9 We also decided to install BMR's control arm brackets. These allow increased adjustment of the rear portion of the control arm for better weight transfer on the track.

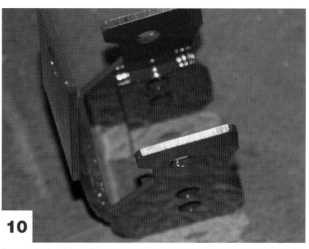

10 Because the brackets will have to be welded in place, you should remove some of the powder coating on the areas where it attaches to the factory brackets.

11 The driver's-side bracket will also anchor to the Panhard rod bolt. The factory unit must be removed, and a new bolt and nut are provided.

12 The BMR adjustable bracket fits over the factory brackets and will bolt in place.

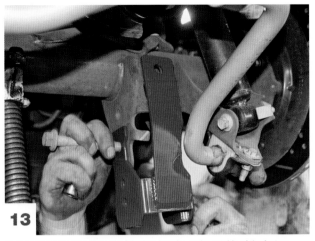

13 On the passenger side, the rear of the bracket sits on the outside of the factory control arm bracket. Both sides are bolted in place using the factory bolt with a spacer that's provided in the kit.

14 We bolted the control arms into position on the top hole. This is a factory setting. The bottom hole will move the vehicle's "instant center" for increased weight transfer for more traction at the drag strip. Once in place, tighten the rod end nuts.

15 The passenger side bracket uses a small bolt and nut to secure it in place on the factory bracket.

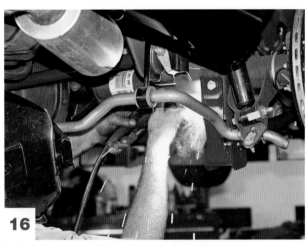

16 The final step is to add a 3-inch weld on both sides of the bracket to ensure it doesn't move under hard acceleration.

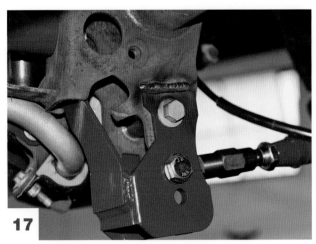

17 Here you can see the bead on the bracket that finishes off our installation.

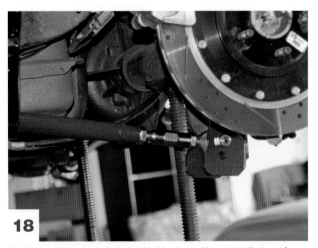

18 This Mustang is ready to gain some added traction and has some adjustment for improved weight transfer when it heads to the drag strip.

SUSPENSION

SECTION 3
BRAKES, WHEELS, AND TIRES

PROJECT 24
Front Brake Upgrade

 High performance brakes on a budget

 Time: 4–6 hours

 Cost: Front and rear kit, $2,000

 Skill level: Moderate; bolt-on with no modifications

 Tools: Requires a torque wrench, line wrench, and fitment template from Baer

When you begin to add some horsepower to your Mustang and have to come down quickly from a high rate of speed, you suddenly realize how poor the factory braking system works. This is one of the reasons why cars from Saleen, Shelby, Roush, and others come equipped with a performance set of six-piston calipers and 14-inch-diameter slotted and drilled rotors. Not only does the extra stopping power allow your Mustang to stop at a shorter distance, but the upgraded components also dissipate heat more quickly and make your braking power much more consistent.

Installing an aftermarket brake kit isn't as expensive as it used to be. There are many options available, including a simple upgrade to performance rotors and pads that can cost less than $500. But a six-piston caliper setup is also easy to install and much more affordable. For this example, a Baer Pro Plus front brake kit works great on 2005–present Mustangs. It offers a six-piston caliper and large rotor package that retails around $1,895, making it much more affordable to give your vehicle some serious brake performance. At the rear, upgrading the rotor to Baer's Eradispeed Plus 2 unit (14-inch rotors) also adds some benefit to the stopping power.

Our brake tests on a 2008 Mustang GT with the factory front and rear brake system averaged a 60-to-0-miles-per-hour stopping distance of 157.11 feet. After the addition of the Pro Plus brakes in the front, along with Baer's Eradispeed

Plus 2 rotor upgrade for the rear, the Mustang improved its 60-to-0 stopping distances by nearly 40 feet and our 100-to-0-miles-per-hour stopping distances by more than 140 feet.*

Because the six-piston Baer 6P calipers are larger, it's a good idea to download the fitment template from the Baer website first. The template will allow you to see if your current wheels will fit over the brakes or if you need a different wheel offset to accommodate the larger calipers. Replacement pads are the same as original equipment in the C5 and C6 Corvette. These pads use the standardized FMSI No. D731 and are readily available in a wide variety of compounds from street to race. They can be found at your local auto parts store.

Aside from adding a supercharger to your Mustang GT, upgrading the brakes actually adds the most performance. They add to your Mustang's intimidation factor too.

*Brake tests done using Stalker Radar Gun in back-to-back comparison tests from 100 miles per hour to 0 and from 60 miles per hour to 0, all done on the same day.

SOURCE

Baer Inc.
3108 W. Thomas Rd., Suite 1201-Q
Phoenix, AZ 85017
(602) 233-1411
www.baer.com

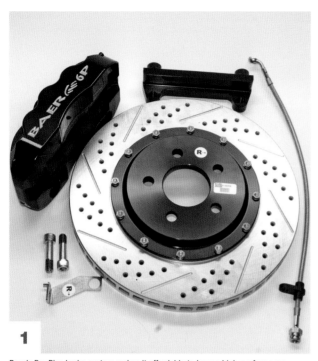

1

Baer's Pro Plus brake system makes it affordable to have a high-performance, six-piston caliper kit on your Mustang GT. It comes with Baer's 6P calipers, 14-inch rotors, steel-braided brake hose, mounting brackets, and hardware.

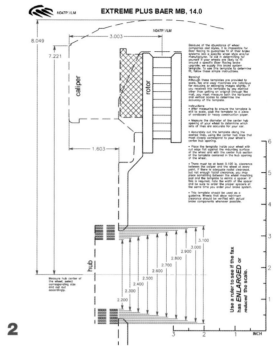

2

From the Baer website, you can download the template to check the fitment of the Pro Plus system on your wheels.

3

Remove the wheel to expose the factory caliper and rotor assembly.

4

Using a line wrench, unbolt the hard brake line from the flexible rubber line that leads to the caliper. Use a small vacuum plug to prevent brake fluid from dripping out, because it could drain the master cylinder reservoir.

5

Behind the shock absorber, there's a brake line bracket that also holds the ABS wiring. This must be removed because a new brake line will be added.

6

The two caliper bolts behind the wheel hub are removed to release the factory caliper. You can then remove the caliper, with the brake hose attached, and pull off the rotor from the hub.

7

Wipe off any dirt or debris from the caliper mounting face and install the new caliper bracket to the hub using the factory bolts. Then tighten the bolts to 85 lbs-ft using a torque wrench.

8

Slide the new rotors onto the hub. Note, there is one labeled "Right" and one labeled "Left." Then install the 6P caliper, with the brake pads in place, onto the bracket using the provided hardware. These bolts must also be tightened to 85 lbs-ft.

9

The new brake line is then installed onto the caliper. The bolt holding the banjo fitting should be tightened to 15–20 lbs-ft. Make sure that the two brass washers are in place between the fitting to avoid any leaks and prevent damage to the caliper.

10

A mounting bracket on the new brake line allows you to attach the hose to the factory location on the shock.

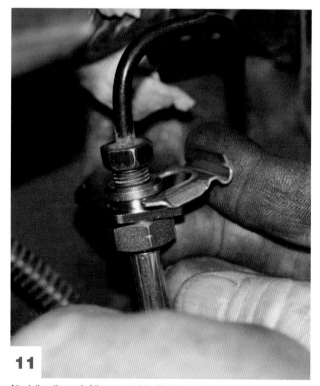

11

Attach the other end of the new steel-braided brake hose to the factory hard brake line with a line wrench. A new bracket replaces the factory unit, and the assembly is secured with the factory clip.

12

The finished installation of the front brakes looks great. Note that the direction the rotor slots are pointing should match the side they are mounted on.

PROJECT 25
Rear Brake Upgrade

 High performance brakes on a budget

 Time: 4–6 hours

 Cost: Front and rear kit, $2,000

 Skill level: Moderate; bolt-on with no modifications

 Tools: Requires a torque wrench, line wrench, and fitment template from Baer

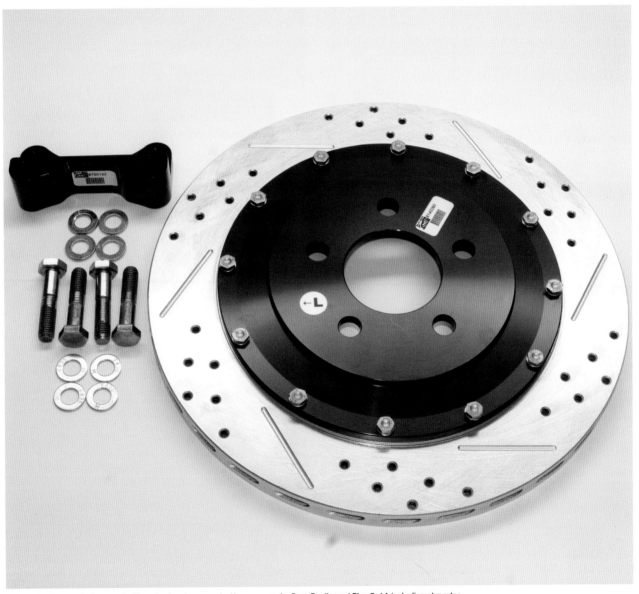

The rear brakes can be improved with a simple rotor upgrade. Here, we used a Baer Eradispeed Plus 2, 14-inch-diameter rotor.

1 The rear calipers are unbolted from behind the hub. A 15mm socket wrench is used to loosen and remove the bolts.

2 Remove the factory caliper and place it out of the way. Then slide off the OEM rotor from the hub.

3 The new caliper mounting bracket is installed using the factory bolts, which are then tightened to 85 lbs-ft.

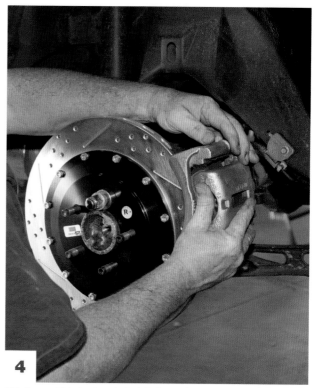

4 Slide the new 14-inch rotor onto the hub, then replace the factory caliper. You may need to use a caliper piston tool to push back the brake piston if the assembly doesn't fit over the rotor.

BRAKES, WHEELS, AND TIRES

Bolt the OEM caliper into its position on the mounting bracket with the hardware provided in the kit.

5

The rear brakes on this Mustang GT now match the front, and the improved rotor material will increase the bite on the pads to help stop the vehicle quicker.

6

In this application, we upgraded the Mustang's wheels to a set of 20×9-inch Shelby Razor aluminum wheels with a 6.5-inch backspacing. They fit perfectly over the factory rear and the larger Baer 6P calipers up front.

7

BRAKES, WHEELS, AND TIRES

111

PROJECT 26
Adding Wheels and Performance Tires

 Fitment and popular sizes for S197 Mustangs

 Time: 45 minutes

 Cost: Varies; $1,200 to $5,000, depending on brand of wheels and tires

 Skill level: Easy to install; must use tire shop to mount and balance

 Tools: Torque wrench required

The right set of wheels and tires on your Mustang is typically a hefty investment. The benefits, however, are great. Not only does a new set of wheels and tires make your Mustang look better, it can also make it perform better.

There's a wide variety of wheels that can be used on 2005-and-later Mustangs. The style is left to your personal taste, but sizing is another matter. Unless you've done some serious bodywork or added a wide-body kit, there's limited space in the vehicle's wheelwells to fit larger or wider tires.

By taking careful measurements and knowing what suspension modifications you will be doing to your Mustang in the future, you'll end up with the right sizes and look

that will make the most of your Mustang's handling and acceleration performance.

SOURCES

Shelby Performance Parts LLC
130 Cassia Way
Henderson, NV 89014
(702) 405-3500
www.shelbyperformanceparts.com

Toyo Tires USA
6261 Katella Ave., Suite 2B
Cypress, CA 90630
(800) 678-3250
www.toyo.com

A mean burnout looks great, but it also says you're losing traction. The right size rubber can gain you an advantage in appearance, handling, and acceleration.

BRAKES, WHEELS, AND TIRES

Factory wheels and tires have changed since 2005. The S197 Mustangs have moved from 18-inch-diameter wheels to 20-inch sizes with the 2010 model.

Many enthusiasts are happy to stay within the 18-inch-diameter range. This has some advantages, since it means you have a better selection of tires and wheels available for street or racing use.

Aftermarket wheels also enhance the look of your Mustang, but to stick wide tires in the front and rear, you'll need to know what backspacing (or wheel offsets) work best.

If you're lowering your vehicle and want to use the widest rubber you can fit, you'll need to take careful measurements. This Mustang is lowered 2 inches and uses a set of 20-inch wheels mounted on 275/35ZR20 Nitto tires. Note how the sidewall comes right to the edge of the vehicle's fenders. This requires the right backspacing for the proper fitment.

1

The best place to start measuring is by using the factory wheels that came with your vehicle. Use a straight edge or straight piece of wood to get a general idea of the wheel's backspacing. This factory 18×8.5-inch wheel that came optional on all 2006–2009 Mustangs has a 6.87-inch backspacing (or 50mm offset from the center of the wheel to the outer lip).

2

The front has some critical areas that dictate a maximum width of tire, no matter if it's an 18- or 20-inch wheel. These important areas are the strut, the bottom edges of the wheelwell, and the front sway bar. The maximum recommended tire width for the front of 2005-and-later Mustangs is a 255/35ZR18 or 20-inch tire. Depending on the width of the wheel, the proper backspacing can range from 6 to 7 inches.

3

Most Mustangs will run front tires with an 8.5- or 9-inch-width wheel. As an example, this lowered Mustang uses a 245/40ZR20 on the front, mounted on a 20×9-inch wheel with a 6-inch backspacing. You can fit a 275/35ZR20 tire, but you'll be limited as to amount you can lower the vehicle.

4

For this fitment example, we decided to use a set of Shelby Razor wheels, available from Shelby Performance Parts and American Racing Wheels. These wheels come in 18- and 20-inch sizes. We used a 20×9 with a 6-inch backspacing (24mm offset) for the front, and a 20×9 with a 6.5-inch backspacing (40mm offset) at the rear.

5

We checked the spacing on the front wheels, and they did measure out to a 6-inch backspacing, preventing any rubbing. Some Mustang models come from the factory with a 17-inch wheel. If you're using an 18- or 20-inch wheel, you'll need to use the Ford Racing steering stop No. 6R3Z3932-CA.

6

If you're using larger brakes, it's also important to check to see if they clear the calipers. Our Shelby Razor wheels cleared the Baer brakes on this application.

7

We mounted the 20×9 Shelby Razor wheels on a set of Toyo Proxes 4, 255/35ZR20 tires. This added some extra width and didn't cause any rubbing problems, even though the vehicle is lowered 1 inch in the front.

8

Some vehicles, such as this Saleen S302 Extreme, use a 20×10-inch wheel with a 305/30ZR20 tire at the rear. But this car needs a custom wheel backspacing of 7.5 inches and an adjustable Panhard bar or Watts link to ensure that it fits properly.

9

We measured 8.5 inches from the mounting point at the rear disc brake hub to the closest point on the wheelwell. This gives us plenty of room to run a 275/35ZR20 (20-inch) tire on a 9-inch rim, as long as we use a 6.5-inch backspacing.

10

We double-checked our Shelby Razor wheels, and they did measure out to a 6.5-inch backspacing, making them perfect for our application.

11

The Toyo Proxes 4 was available in a 275/40ZR20, which gave us a ½-inch-taller tire for additional traction on acceleration. But you can also use a 35-series tire that would better level out the stance of the vehicle.

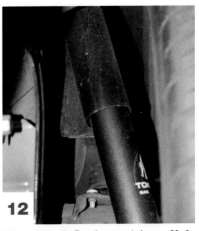

12

With our 275-series Toyo tires mounted on our 20×9-inch Shelby Razor wheels, you can see that there's plenty of room between the inside wheelwell and shock and the tire sidewall.

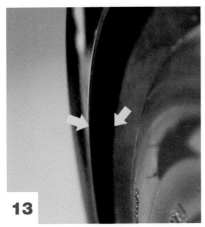

13

When running a larger tire in the rear, you have to carefully note the gap between the fender lip and the tire sidewall.

14

To ensure that the axle stays centered and that the wheelwell lip-to-tire sidewall space remains equal, you'll need an adjustable Panhard rod. This will allow you to make small adjustments and to keep the sidewalls from rubbing the fender lip during hard cornering.

A tire like this Yokohama Advan is an example of a new breed of "Grand Touring" tire that combines the best of a performance tire and a touring tire in one.

New tire technologies are bridging the gap between performance and all-season tires. The Yokohama Advan for example features large shoulder blocks that add tread stiffness and increase handling, multi-directional sipes to improve all-season performance, and three large center grooves to quickly expel water.

Compared side by side, the Yokohama Advan grand touring tire on the left features many of the same components as the ultra high performance Toyo Proxes T1R tire on the right. The differences in compounds make the Toyo T1R superior in dry traction, but the added sripes and grooves on the Yokohama Advan make it a superior all-season tire. So it's important to factor this into your thinking when making a tire purchase for your Mustang.

Choose your tires carefully. Some provide excellent high-performance traction with good street durability, such as these Toyo Proxes 4s. They are mud- and snow-rated tires that are an example of ultra-high performance, providing improved traction and handling for vehicles like our Mustang.

If you want higher performance and are willing to sacrifice some performance in mud and snow, then a tire like this Toyo T1R offers extreme performance for higher-powered Mustangs with extensive suspension modifications.

For those people who are ready to race their Mustangs at any given moment, or who take their vehicles to the autocross or drag strip, a street/strip tire that's Department of Transportation (DOT) legal is required. This Toyo R1R is a perfect example, with a softer racing rubber compound, yet it has treads to keep the tire quiet and stable and is only available in 18-inch-diameter sizes.

BRAKES, WHEELS, AND TIRES

116

SECTION 4
DRIVETRAIN

PROJECT 27
Adding a High-Performance Clutch

 Higher horsepower requires a performance clutch upgrade

 Time: 6–8 hours

Cost: $850 (parts)

 Skill level: Experienced

 Tools: No special tools; requires a torque wrench and clutch alignment tool

As you increase the horsepower and torque in your Mustang GT, the factory clutch will begin to slip and lose power. The Ford 3650 five-speed transmission has a clutch that is rated around 350–400 lbs-ft of torque. Simply adding a supercharger or nitrous oxide will get you beyond the level of the factory clutch's holding capacity. But selecting the right aftermarket clutch can be a little tricky. The amount of rear-wheel torque should determine which type of clutch you need, ranging from a high-performance street clutch to a dual-friction design or even a puck-style racing model. Obviously, the more torque your engine makes, the more clamping force you'll need.

Fortunately, replacing the clutch is the same no matter if it's a stock replacement or a full race clutch. The process of removing and replacing the Mustang's clutch is straightforward and is much easier to perform if you have access to a lift and a transmission jack. The transmission is unbolted from the engine block around the bellhousing. In addition, you'll have to unbolt the exhaust from the factory manifolds and move them out of the way. Make sure to also unplug all of the connections to the oxygen sensors and all the wiring connections that lead to the transmission, shift linkage, and front driveshaft. The hydraulic line that connects to a fitting in the transmission's bellhousing must also be unplugged. Manufacturers like Centerforce provide a small line plug that prevents all the fluid from draining out of the clutch reservoir.

In this application, we installed a Centerforce DFX clutch, pressure plate, and SFI-approved billet flywheel combination. This particular Mustang makes more than 500 horsepower to the rear wheels, and the DFX street/strip-designed clutch has enough clamping force for this engine. While it does sacrifice a little street smoothness (shutters a little when starting in first gear), the DFX doesn't let an ounce of torque slip when it's engaged. We also modified the hydraulic line to improve the quickness of the throw-out bearing action. This results in extremely quick shifts without a heavy clutch pedal effort and the ability to launch hard without slipping. The combination also didn't hinder our street driving at all, allowing this Mustang to be driven sedately on the street or hard at the track.

SOURCE

Centerforce Clutches
2266 Crosswind Drive.
Prescott, AZ 86301
(928) 771-8422
www.centerforce.com

The factory Mustang five-speed transmission can handle good amounts of power, but the factory clutch must be upgraded to handle more than 400 lbs-ft of torque.

DRIVETRAIN

118

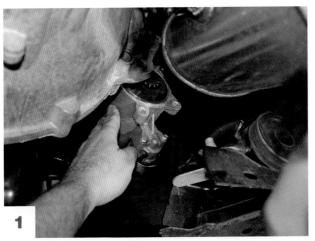

1

To upgrade the clutch, you first need to remove the factory starter and unplug all of the wiring to the transmission and oxygen sensors.

2

Unbolting the exhaust from the catalytic converters allows for extra room that's required to remove the transmission. Here you can see that a stand is used to support the transmission once the crossmember is unbolted from the chassis.

3

The driveshaft will have to be disconnected from each end. The center driveshaft bearing is also removed.

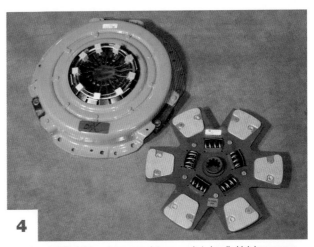

4

Centerforce's DFX clutch and pressure plate are made to handle high horsepower and torque. The six-puck-style clutch has superior grip, and the pressure plate uses a ball-bearing-actuated diaphragm for superior holding power with less pedal effort.

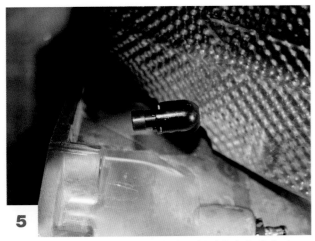

5

The last step before removing the transmission is to detach the hydraulic line from the master cylinder. Centerforce uses a plug to keep the fluid from pouring out of the cylinder reservoir.

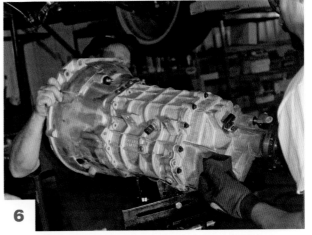

6

All the bolts that secure the transmission bellhousing to the engine block are removed, and a trans jack is used to carefully lower the transmission out of the vehicle.

DRIVETRAIN

7

The factory clutch and pressure plate can then be unbolted from the OEM flywheel.

8

This factory flywheel is in good shape, but we'll be replacing it with a Centerforce, SFI-approved billet unit that is much stronger and safer.

9

Here, you can see the differences in the two types of clutches and materials. The factory clutch on the left has a smoother operation but less adhesion. The DFX clutch on the right is a racing-style, six-puck design that has less slippage and grips faster. It's used for higher-horsepower applications and is great for street/strip use.

10

The hydraulic actuator for the throw-out bearing is unbolted from the front of the transmission.

11

Centerforce provides a shim that fits behind the actuator. This allows for proper spacing between the throw-out bearing and the fingers of the pressure plate.

12

The Centerforce pressure plate on the left uses the company's unique centrifugal weights on the pressure plate fingers. This adds holding power without any unnecessary pedal pressure.

DRIVETRAIN

13 Here, we bolt on the Centerforce, SFI-approved billet flywheel. Note the dowel pins on the flywheel used to further secure and center the pressure plate.

14 The clutch plate is held in place with a clutch-centering tool.

15 Then the pressure plate is bolted on top, making sure the alignment is perfectly centered.

16 Will Baty of Centerforce shows us how to modify the Mustang's factory hydraulic line fittings with a ⁷⁄₆₄ drill bit. High-pressure air is blown into the line from the opposite side to remove any metal shavings that may have been left inside.

17 The opposite side of the hydraulic line can be removed, and it too is drilled using the ⁷⁄₆₄ drill bit. This modification will provide quicker flow of fluid to the hydraulic throw-out bearing for faster actuation.

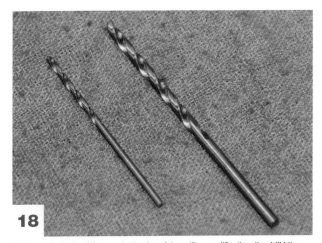

18 To demonstrate the difference in the size of the orifice modification, the drill bit on the bottom is the size of the factory orifice. The drill bit on top is the ⁷⁄₆₄ drill bit used to modify the line.

Installing a Performance Short-Throw Shifter

 Gearing up

 Time: 3 hours

$ **Cost:** $190–$300 (shifter or shifter plus knob)

★ **Skill level:** Easy; can be done by a novice

Tools: No special tools; requires metric and standard socket and open-end wrenches; access to a lift and friend may be helpful to make the job easier

A short-throw shifter is a must for any Mustang with a manual transmission. It allows for quicker and more precise shifting that makes it much more enjoyable to bang through the gears. Because the S197 Mustang uses an external-mounted shifter, there's a tendency for additional transmission noise and binding that can occur if the geometry isn't perfect. That's why you need to look for an aftermarket unit that can eliminate any flexing of the shifter body and mount with a strong support arm. The shifter lever must also be properly insulated to reduce vibrations that can be translated from the transmission.

We found this Shelby Performance shifter (No. 7S3Z-7210-F5) to be an excellent performance upgrade. It features a sturdy design that's manufactured from 6061-T6 billet aluminum, which makes this unit both lightweight and strong. When used in conjunction with high-durometer polyurethane bushings, it eliminates any flexing of the shifter support arm under hard acceleration for more precise and smooth shifts.

When installing any aftermarket shifter into an S197 Mustang GT, one can never be sure about the clearance between the front shifter mount that attaches to the transmission and the transmission tunnel sheet metal. Almost all Mustangs are built differently, and in some cases,

there's enough room to remove the shifter support arm bolt (without having to remove the crossmember) and lower the transmission an inch or two to remove the bolt. If you're not sure, follow the directions, because most give great detail about how to accomplish this.

In some cases, it's also unnecessary to remove the front driveshaft from the input shaft of the transmission. But if you do, it allows much more freedom of movement to unbolt the shifter lever from the transmission shift linkage. In addition, the rear of the factory shifter mount is secured with two studs mounted directly to the sheet metal. Be careful not to damage the studs because they can easily break and are extremely difficult to replace. Installing any shifter is an easy task that yields improved shifting, precise control, and, in some cases, an improved look to your Mustang's center console.

SOURCE

Shelby Performance Parts LLC
130 Cassia Way
Henderson, NV 89014
(702) 405-3500
www.shelbyperformanceparts.com

Adding a performance short-throw shifter improves the appearance of your Mustang's interior, as well as improving your shifting pleasure and performance.

This Shelby Performance Parts shifter comes disassembled with all of the pieces shown here. The main features are the billet aluminum transmission mount, injected Delrin pivot cup, and polyurethane bushings and sleeves.

For normal driving, the factory shifter looks great, but it feels heavy and has a long shift throw, which doesn't make it good for performance shifting.

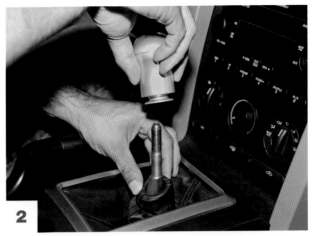

Pull back on the boot and simply unscrew the factory shifter knob.

The boot and frame are removed by unclipping them from the console. You're then left with the factory shifter lever and inner rubber insulation.

From underneath the car, unbolt the front driveshaft from the transmission's input shaft. This requires removing the four bolts and allowing the driveshaft to drop out of the way. Note how we marked the driveshaft and input shaft so that we can replace it in the exact position.

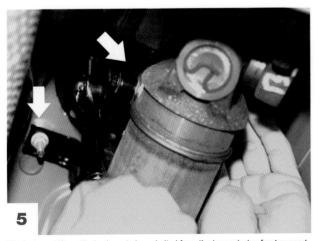

The factory shifter will also have to be unbolted from the transmission front support arm, shift linkage, and rear mount as shown here.

Once everything is unbolted from the factory shifter, it can be removed either from inside the cab or from underneath.

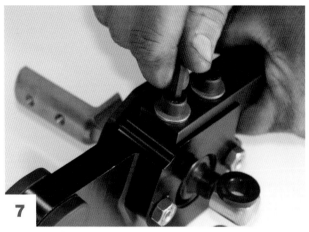

7

This Shelby Performance shifter is assembled by first attaching the front support arm mount to the main body of the shifter. Some shifters have the support arm already attached.

8

The rear mount is also assembled using the steel mounts that sandwich the polyurethane bushings in between to reduce vibrations. Other shifters may use a single polyurethane bushing that straddles the rear shifter assembly.

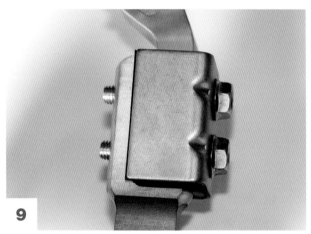

9

The billet shifter lever is attached to the pivot lever using these two bolts. What you don't see are the urethane bolt polyurethane inner and outer sleeve that keep vibration from coming up through the lever.

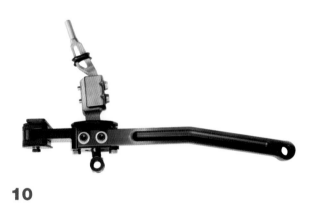

10

The assembled shifter is now ready to be installed into the Mustang from under the vehicle.

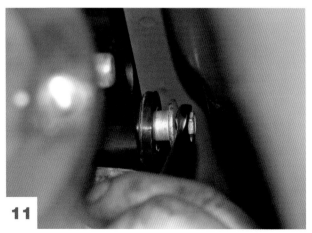

11

We were lucky that the front shifter support arm mount bolt fit into position without having to lower the transmission. You can see how tight it is between the bolt and the trans tunnel.

12

The rear of the shifter is bolted to the factory studs. Be sure not to over-tighten them because they can sheer off from the body.

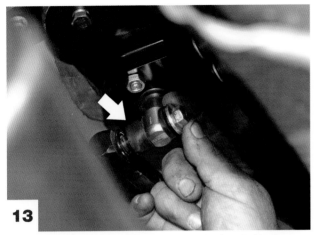

13

It's important to make sure the bushings are set correctly when attaching the transmission linkage to the shift lever. The large bushing fits on the driver's side against the linkage arm.

14

Following the directions, adjust the shift stops to prevent overextension of the shifter arms and lock them in place.

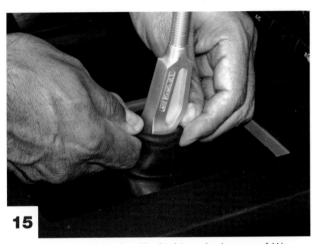

15

From inside the cab, reposition the rubber insulator, and make sure you fold in the top around the shift lever. This prevents any transmission sound from entering the cab.

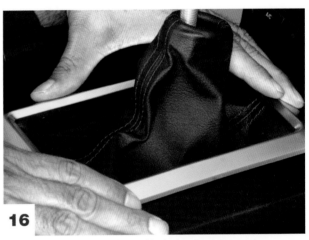

16

Reinstall the boot by pressing it into position back on the center console.

17

The Shelby Performance shifter comes with a new shifter ring that correctly sets the boot around the new shifter lever.

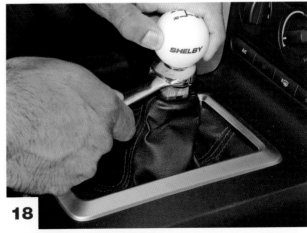

18

The final touch is to add the white shift knob, sold separately, onto the shifter and secure it in place with the lock nut.

PROJECT 29
Installing a Ratchet Automatic Shifter

 Positive intent

 Time: 1–2 hours

$ Cost: $350

Skill level: Easy; can be done by a novice

Tools: No special tools; requires metric and standard socket and open-end wrenches; access to a lift makes the job easier

Mustangs equipped with the factory 5R55S utilize an automatic transmission shifter that leaves much to be desired for street/strip performance. Many Mustang owners prefer a ratchet-style shifter that features a positive stop action to eliminate the risk of neutral mis-shifts when shifting up through the gears in a manual mode. Fortunately, there are direct bolt-in replacements that feature drag-racing functions, such as a reverse lockout, that improve the performance and appearance of your Mustang's interior.

We installed the TCI StreetFighter shifter that fits all S197 Mustangs equipped with the 5R55S automatic transmission.

The installation is simple, but there are some important steps that must be taken when removing and reinstalling the factory shifter cable to ensure proper operation after the new shifter is installed.

SOURCE

TCI Automotive
151 Industrial Drive
Ashland, MS 38603
(888) 776-9824
www.tciauto.com

This ratchet shifter from TCI is an example of a performance automatic shifter with a reverse lockout mechanism that's perfect for street/strip use.

Move the factory shifter into the DRIVE position and apply the parking brake. Disconnect the negative battery terminal, then raise the vehicle. If you don't have access to a lift, secure the vehicle with jack stands.

Gently pry on both sides of the shifter bevel and remove the top of the center console by removing the screws toward the rear (under the armrest). Gently work it over the parking brake arm to remove it from the vehicle.

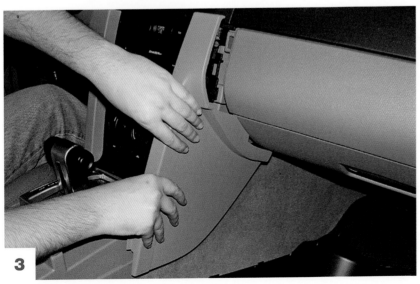

Remove the side panels of the center console by simply pulling them back and up. These are located under the dash at the front of the console.

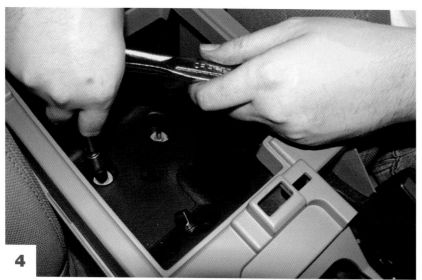

With the side panels out, remove the two screws at the front of the console and the two nuts located under the armrest inside the storage area. If there is a power outlet in the rear of the console, make sure you unplug it before removing the console!

4

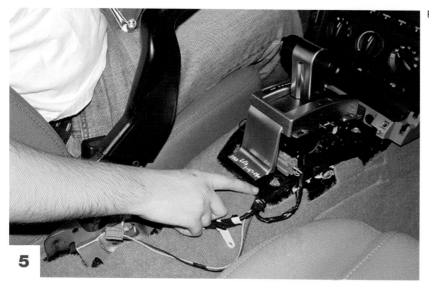

Remove the center console to expose the shifter.

5

From under the vehicle, use a flathead screwdriver to pry up the tab inside the sliding lock that secures the connector to the shift arm. With the screwdriver held on the tab, slide the tab up to unlock the connector. From there, gently pry the shift cable away from the lever.

6

Moving up the shifter cable, you'll come to a bracket with a locking clip. There are two small holes on the cable support bracket that keep the locking clip attached. Look at the TCI shifter to understand how the cable is mounted. Next, press the lower locking ear on the connector through the small hole in the bracket using a small screwdriver, and at the same time push up on the small tab. Do the same with the upper locking ear and tab. If you can't get the upper tab to release, gently pry the shifter cable from the bracket using a screwdriver.

From inside the car, remove the two bolts and two nuts located on the outside corners of the shifter. Unplug the plug from the rear passenger side of the shifter and pull it to the side. Now you can remove the shifter.

Insert the new TCI StreetFighter ratchet shifter and carefully run down and snug the two bolts and two nuts using a "crisscross" pattern. THIS IS VERY IMPORTANT! With a torque wrench, torque them down evenly to 80 lbs-in using the same crisscross pattern. If this is not done correctly, you can damage the shifter.

DRIVETRAIN

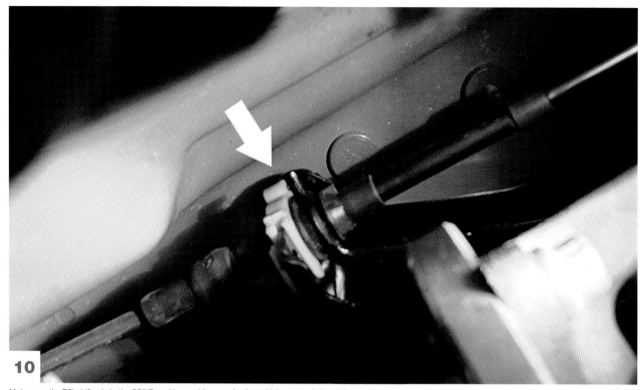

10

Make sure the TCI shifter is in the DRIVE position, and from under the vehicle, reattach the shifter cable to the cable support bracket.

11

Carefully align the shifter cable end with the shift arm attachment. Make sure you allow the sliding tab to align itself. If you even slightly force the cable in or out, the shifter will not function properly. After attaching the connector to the shifter arm, lock the cable into position by lowering the sliding lock. Put the shifter in the PARK position and reconnect the battery cables. Turn on the ignition key and verify that the shift indicator shows an amber LED light in PARK only and that it moves smoothly from PARK through each gear. Reinstall the center console, side panels, and shifter bezel.

PROJECT 30
Installing a Performance Torque Converter

 A quick reaction

 Time: 5–6 hours

 Cost: $550

 Skill level: Moderate to difficult; simple to bolt on but requires a working knowledge of automatic transmissions

 Tools: No special tools; requires hydraulic lift, transmission floor jack, and torque wrench

When your Mustang's engine horsepower increases, the factory automatic transmission also needs to follow along, or there's a mismatch that can result in lost performance. Upgrading the OEM torque converter to a performance unit with a slightly higher stall speed will improve the reaction and quickness of your Mustang, allowing you to take advantage of your engine's increased power and giving you improved quarter-mile time slips.

Aftermarket torque converters like TCI's StreetFighter will multiply torque through a redesigned stator that delivers as much as a 2.5 to 1 torque increase. The increased torque multiplication of the converter results in quicker 60-foot acceleration times and shifting efficiency.

The TCI StreetFighter No. 456000 is made for 2005–2006 Mustang GTs equipped with the 4.6-liter V-8 and 5R55 automatic transmission. The converter has a 3,000-rpm stall speed (over the factory 2,500 stall) and installs using the factory flex plate. The result of this installation was nearly half a second shaved off the quarter-mile times of this stock Mustang GT.

SOURCE

TCI Automotive
151 Industrial Drive
Ashland, MS 38603
(888) 776-9824
www.tciauto.com

The TCI StreetFighter torque converter has a 3,000-rpm stall speed and improves acceleration times with better torque multiplication over the factory converter's 2,500-rpm stall speed.

DRIVETRAIN

131

1

This 2006 Ford Mustang ran the quarter mile in 14.35 seconds at 97.05 miles per hour. On the Comp Cams dyno, it showed 250 horsepower and 240 lbs-ft of torque. After the torque converter upgrade, it ran 13.94 seconds at 96.45 miles per hour, shaving off nearly a half-second from its quarter-mile time.

2

The converter swap begins by unhooking the negative-side battery cable.

3

The driveshaft is unbolted from the rear of the transmission and then the rear-mounted hoop. Move it out of the way to provide clearance and allow the transmission to be lowered.

4

On the 2005-and-newer Mustangs equipped with the 5R55 transmission, it isn't mandatory to drain the transmission oil. However, you will need to refill the transmission once the new converter is installed because of the fluid lost during removal of the converter and the cooler lines. This transmission does not have a transmission fill tube, so fluid must be pumped up into the transmission through this fitting to refill the pan.

5

Unplug the oxygen sensors from the underside of the transmission body that attach to the main wiring harness.

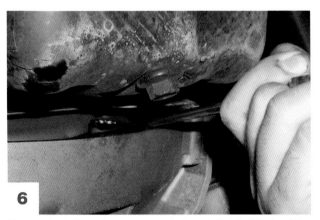

6

After removing the inspection cover, remove the four nuts that attach the flex plate to the torque converter mounting plate. All four nuts must be removed. You'll have to reconnect the battery to bump the engine over to reach all four bolts.

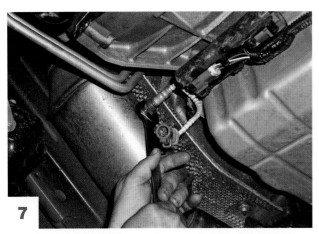

7

Using a 22mm wrench, carefully remove the sensors from the exhaust to avoid damaging them.

8

Unbolt the transmission cooler lines with a line wrench, making certain not to bend them or strip the line fittings. The cooler lines will leak fluid once you unhook them, so be ready with a catch pan.

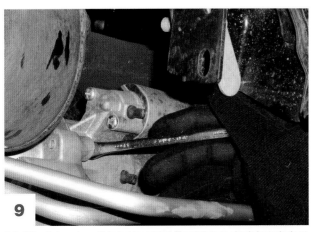

9

Unbolt the starter using a ¼-inch drive ratchet. The starter can simply be tucked out of the way to provide enough clearance to lower the transmission.

10

Using a long extension, remove the bellhousing bolts. Position a transmission jack underneath and unbolt the exhaust system at the catalytic converters and the rear crossmember. Then, slowly lower the transmission to provide enough clearance to reach the upper bellhousing bolts.

11

Be especially careful with the transmission linkage system when unclipping it, noting the original position of these parts.

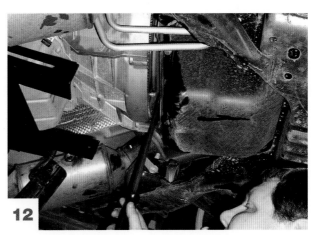

12

Carefully pry the flex plate away from the back of the engine. The studs protruding from the torque converter mounting plate have a tendency to catch on the back of the engine.

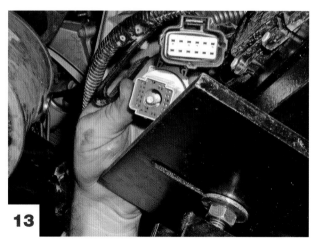

13

The transmission has a number of connections to be found on the passenger side of the unit. Carefully unscrew the main connector from the housing and unclip the other sensor connections.

14

With all of the connections undone, lower the transmission, making certain it is carefully balanced (attaching it to the jack with straps is a good idea). Be careful not to damage the transmission lines on the way down.

15

With the transmission finally free from the car, remove the torque converter by pulling it straight out. It will be heavy and filled with fluid.

16

The converter holds approximately 3.5 to 4 quarts of oil. Once it is out of the vehicle, drain the converter in a catch pan.

17

Unbolt the torque converter mounting plate from the old converter.

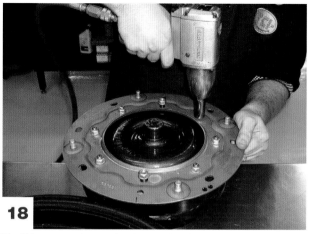

18

The old torque converter mounting plate must be bolted to the new TCI StreetFighter torque converter. Use the same nuts used by the factory to reinstall the flex plate, and torque them to factory specs.

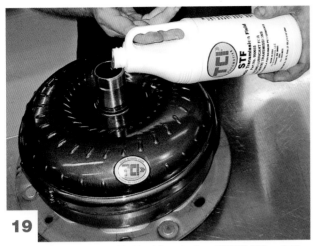

19

Fill the new torque converter with at least 2 quarts of new TCI MAX-Shift synthetic transmission fluid.

20

Lift the converter onto the snout and twist it until it sits correctly on the input shaft (you'll hear it go into position). Then lift the transmission back into its position and bolt it back onto the engine.

Reinstall the oxygen sensors. Make certain that the coverings are in the right place and that the wiring is situated so that it cannot come in contact with other parts or catch on road hazards.

21

Without question, this is the most frustrating pan fill system we've ever encountered. Without a fill tube, you must pump the oil up through the center of the oil drain plug to fill this transmission. The inner tube in the drain plug sets the fluid level. Once the oil in the pan has reached the correct level, the fluid will drain back out of the center tube. In order to properly fill the car, it must be idling in park and be level. Make certain that the main drain plug is snugged up, fill the system, and then reinsert the center Torx-headed plug.

22

PROJECT 31
Adding a Driveshaft Safety Loop

 A safe bet

 Time: 1 hour

Cost: $190, depending on product

 Skill level: Easy; beginner can install by following the instructions

 Tools: No special tools required; standard and metric socket wrench set will be used

Once you start adding some serious horsepower to your S197 Mustang, it places a higher load on the factory drivetrain. Since the driveshaft is typically one of the weakest links in the chain, most enthusiasts want to prevent it from breaking and damaging the vehicle's underside as well as other drivetrain components.

A single-piece driveshaft is great, but it can also be expensive and often requires you to adjust the pinion angle of your differential. A much easier and less expensive alternative is to install a dual driveshaft safety loop system. A heavy-duty steel safety loop system for the late-model S195 Mustang, like the one we installed from Granatelli Motorsports, can eliminate the chance of damage should one or both sections of the factory driveshafts break.

The Granatelli Motorsports driveshaft safety loop system for the S197 Mustang mounts to within 6 inches of the U-joints and surrounds the driveshafts to meet National Hot Rod Association (NHRA) rules. So, if you ever plan on doing any kind of performance testing with your Mustang on the quarter-mile strip, keep in mind that some tracks require driveshaft safety loops for rear-axle cars running 13.99 with slicks and 13.0 with street tires. Even if you plan to test your Mustang on the dyno, there's always comfort in knowing you've taken extra safety precautions.

SOURCE

Granatelli Motorsports
1000 Yarnell Place
Oxnard, CA 93033
(804) 466-6644
www.granatellimotorsports.com

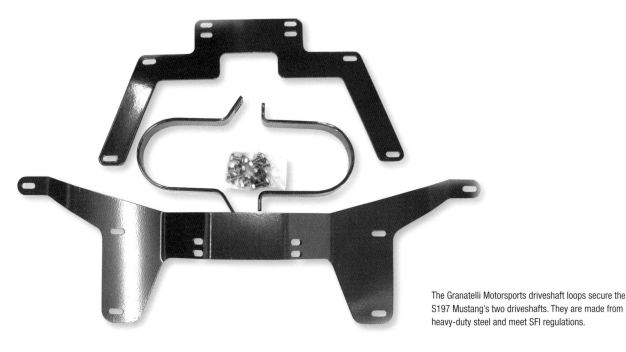

The Granatelli Motorsports driveshaft loops secure the S197 Mustang's two driveshafts. They are made from heavy-duty steel and meet SFI regulations.

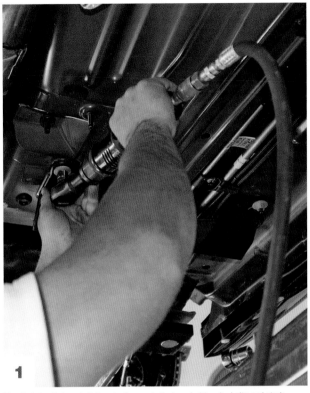

1

The first step is to unbolt the plastic panels that are held on by bolts and studs under the vehicle.

2

Factory heat shields that are closer to the engine are also removed. These also use studs and bolts.

3

To make more working space between the body and the exhaust, you can unbolt the sleeves for the factory H-pipe and move it out of the way.

4

Both the front and rear driveshaft loop braces slip over the exhaust and match the bolt holes and studs under the floorpan.

Here, you can see how the driveshaft loop braces fit onto the factory floorpan.

5

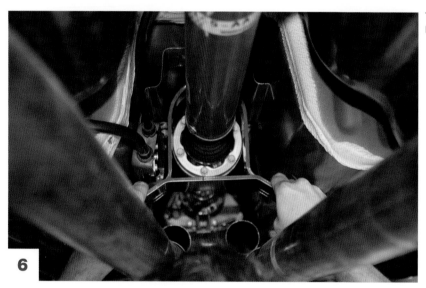

The safety loops fit over the driveshaft and bolt onto the braces with the provided hardware.

6

Installation takes about an hour, and once you're done, you've got good insurance against severe damage should one of the driveshafts come loose during a dyno run or track testing.

7

DRIVETRAIN

SECTION 5
BODY AND EXTERIOR

PROJECT 32
Body Kit Upgrade: Bumper

? Adding complete style to a V-6 Mustang

Time: 3–4 hours

$ **Cost:** $299.99, cost of complete body kit (not including prep and paint)

★ **Skill level:** Medium; some drilling, modifications, and wiring required

Tools: Standard SAE and metric tools, drill, and bit set; wire cutters and crimping tool

Many Mustang owners choose to customize the exterior of their cars piece by piece, picking out various parts from different manufacturers. However, one of the best ways to change the appearance of your Mustang while keeping a uniform look is to install a full body kit. They come in a variety of styles and materials, and they range from just a front and rear fascia to full-blown kits that include a new rear spoiler, grille, hood, side skirts, and more.

Street Scene Equipment, based in Costa Mesa, California, is a leading supplier for exterior styling accessories for a variety of cars and trucks. The body kit installed on our Mustang is their Generation 1 V-6 complete kit that comes with a new front bumper, side skirts, door fillers, and rear valence. We also added SSE's side scoops and rear spoiler that can be ordered separately. Each of the components is made from flexible urethane, and we found that all of the pieces fit on the car with no problem.

Installing the Street Scene Equipment body kit can take several hours and often requires two people when putting on the larger items like the front bumper, side skirts, and rear valence. While all of our components were already painted at the time of our installation, they generally come unpainted. However, each piece should be test-fit prior to the application of paint or the actual installation. With the exception of the front bumper, which is secured in place using the stock screws and clips, all of the pieces are fitted to the car using a sticky adhesive and double-sided tape. To ensure that each piece fits as securely as possible, it is important to prep each one with sandpaper and make sure that the car is completely clean where the components are being installed. Occasionally, additional screws will also be used to secure the parts onto the car. Also, if a new grille with auxiliary lighting is installed, then some wiring will be required.

SOURCE

Street Scene Equipment
365 McCormick Avenue
Costa Mesa, CA 92626
(714) 426-0590
www.streetsceneeq.com

1 The standard Street Scene Equipment Generation 1 body kit comes with a new front bumper, side skirts, door fillers, and a rear valence. The kit installed on this Mustang also included a new grille with auxiliary lights and a rear spoiler.

2 We started with the installation of the SSE front bumper, which first requires removal of the plastic radiator cover. Simply use a flathead screwdriver to pry out the six plastic fasteners.

BODY AND EXTERIOR

140

Next, remove the two screws on each side of the inner wheelwell. This allows the fender liner to be pulled up, and the three 10mm screws that secure the fascia to the car on each side can be removed.

It takes two to remove the front fascia. However, any lighting, including marker lights or auxiliary fog lights, should be unplugged before it can be taken off.

This brace holds the corner lamps in place, which need to be transferred from the stock fascia to the new one. To remove it, the rivets have to be drilled out.

With the brace transferred to the new front fascia and drilled into position, the corner lamps can be fitted and bolted on.

6

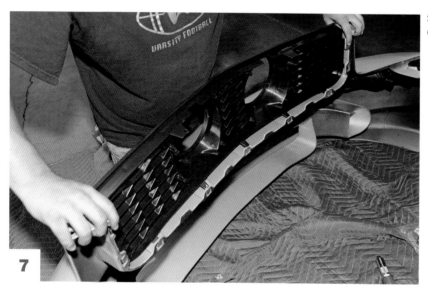

Street Scene Equipment provides a new front grille that easily clips into position on the new front fascia.

7

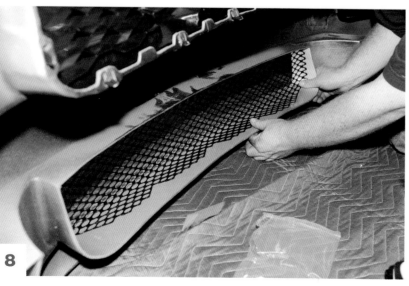

A lower mesh grille also comes with the front fascia. It is important to ensure it is properly lined up before bolting it on.

8

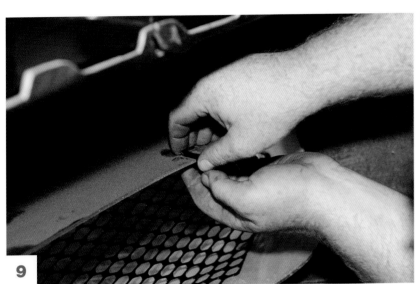

The lower grille can be attached at the top with several clips provided by Street Scene Equipment.

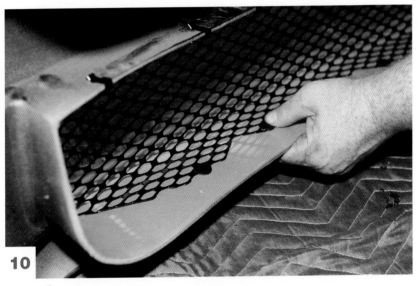

The bottom portion of the lower grille is secured with plastic fasteners that require a small hole to be drilled.

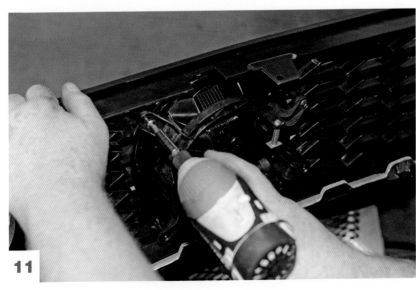

Auxiliary lights come with the kit, and our Mustang doesn't already have them, so we decided to use the new lights. These lights bolt directly into the grille with the screws provided in the kit.

The necessary wiring harnesses for the auxiliary lighting come with the kit. The wiring plugs directly into the back of each light.

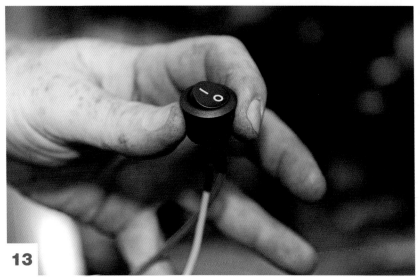

A switch also comes with the lighting system. It can be installed anywhere in the interior.

With the main and lower grille in place, it's time to install the new front fascia. As with the removal of the old unit, this is a two-person job. The three screws on each side that secured the stock piece are reused. So are the two screws that hold the wheelwell liner.

PROJECT 33
Body Kit Upgrade: Side Skirts

? Adding complete style to a V-6 Mustang

★ Skill level: Medium; some drilling and modifications required

🕐 Time: 1–2 hours

🔧 Tools: Standard SAE and metric tools, double-sided tape, and automotive adhesion

$ Cost: $299.99, cost of complete body kit (not including prep and paint)

The next step is to install the side skirts, a step that begins by removing the two plastic fasteners that hold them in place at the front.

With the two plastic fasteners removed, the side skirts are pried from the car. They are attached with more fasteners, which will pop out of place.

BODY AND EXTERIOR

145

Once the stock side skirt is taken off, any of the fasteners that are still connected to the body of the car need to be removed.

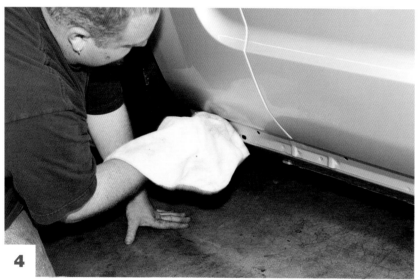

Once the side skirt is completely taken off, the entire area needs to be thoroughly cleaned in preparation for the new piece.

Throughout the rest of the installation, double-sided tape and automotive adhesion will be used to attach the rest of the body kit.

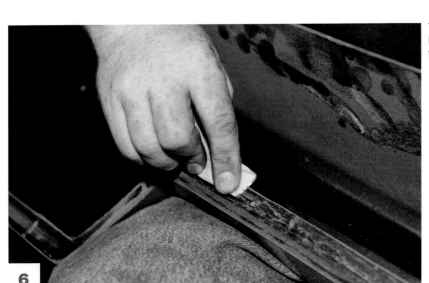

To prepare the new side skirt to be fitted on the car, the inside edges are sanded smooth so that the adhesion and the double-sided tape sticks as much as possible.

Once prepped and with adhesion applied, the two-sided tape is fitted on the inside edge of the side skirt.

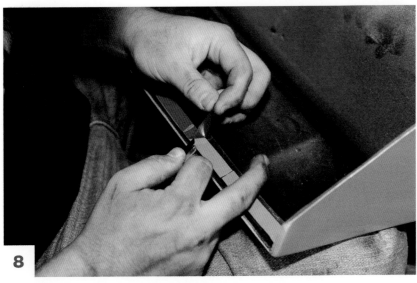

One all the tape is applied to the skirt, the protective covering is pulled back to uncover the sticky side of the tape.

With all the tape uncovered, the side skirt is fitted in place. Because the tape has a strong bond, it is important to make sure that the side skirt is properly positioned before firmly pressing it into place.

9

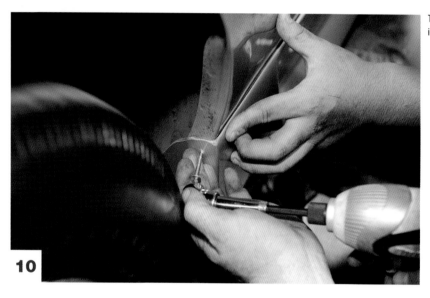

To ensure that the side skirt stays in place, two screws are inserted at the rear.

10

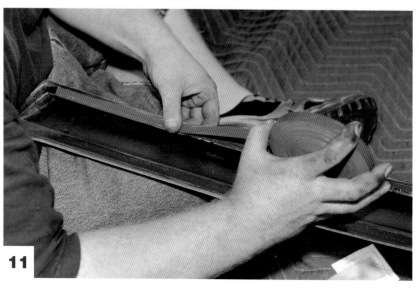

The side skirts require a door filler that needs to be prepared identically. This includes sanding, application of adhesion, and applying the double-sided tape.

11

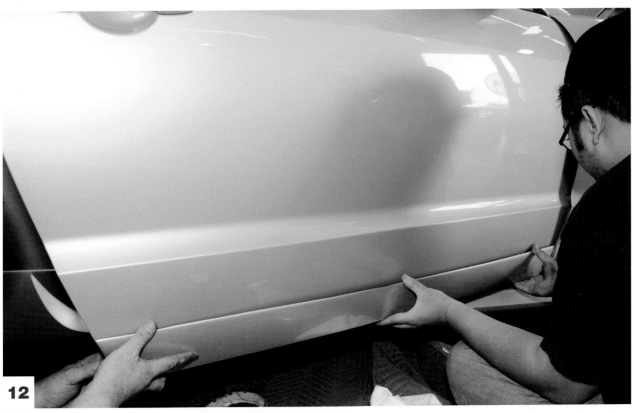

12 With the tape in place, the door filler can be pressed into its final position.

13 Here is a look at the side skirt and door filler completely installed. With care and patience, the fitment will be absolutely perfect.

PROJECT 34
Body Kit Upgrade: Side Scoops

? Adding complete style to a V-6 Mustang

Time: Less than 1 hour

$ Cost: $299.99, cost of complete body kit (not including prep and paint)

★ Skill level: Easy; no modifications required

Tools: Sand paper, double-sided tape, and automotive adhesion

1

The side scoops also need to be prepped before installation. This process includes light sanding, application of adhesion, and application of double-sided tape.

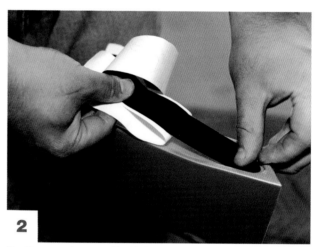

2

The side scoops also come with a black decal that can be applied in the faux opening. The decals are different for each side, so it is important to make sure each one is being applied to the correct side.

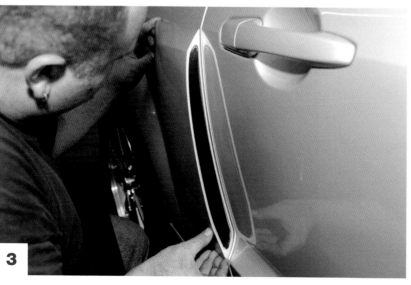

3

The side scoops are installed just behind the door and above the side skirts. Once the proper fitment is found, press firmly into place.

PROJECT 35
Body Kit Upgrade: Rear Valence

? Adding complete style to a V-6 Mustang

🕐 **Time:** 1–2 hours

$ **Cost:** $299.99, cost of complete body kit (not including prep and paint)

⭐ **Skill level:** Medium; some drilling and modifications required

Tools: Standard SAE and metric tools, drill and bit set, sandpaper, double-sided tape, automotive adhesion

1

The rear valence needs to be prepped for installation including sanding and applying the adhesion and double-sided tape on all the inside edges of the piece.

2

Fitting the rear valence into place is a two-person job and requires careful precision to place it in the correct position.

3

While not mandatory, we would recommend using several screws to secure the rear valence to the body.

4

Because our Mustang is a V-6 model, it came with a blocked-out exhaust port on the left side. If you have a V-6 and don't like this look, we would recommend getting a dual exhaust conversion kit and getting the valence with the dual holes.

PROJECT 36
Body Kit Upgrade: Rear Wing

 Adding complete style to a V-6 Mustang

 Skill level: Easy; no modifications required

 Time: 1–2 hours

 Tools: Sandpaper, double-sided tape, automotive adhesion

Cost: $299.99, cost of complete body kit (not including prep and paint)

1

The rear wing comes in three pieces, including two side pieces that attach to the rear fenders. These need to be prepped by sanding and applying adhesion and double-sided tape before installation.

2

Each side piece of the rear wing fits on a corner of the rear fender and needs to be firmly pressed in place.

BODY AND EXTERIOR

152

The center section of the rear wing needs the same preparation as the other pieces.

3

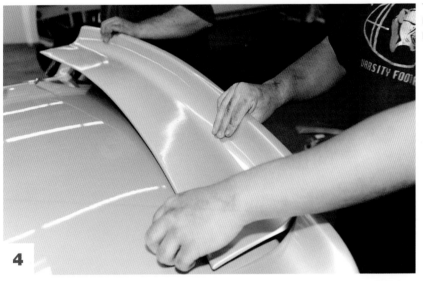

The rear wing fits directly onto the trunk and needs to be pressed firmly into place. We found that it lined up perfectly with the other two pieces of the wing.

4

With the front fascia, side skirts and door fillers, side scoops, rear valence, and rear wing in place, the installation of the body kit is complete. The look of your Mustang has been transformed!

5

BODY AND EXTERIOR

153

PROJECT 37
Performance Hood Upgrade

 Hood transformation

 Time: 72 hours (includes prep and paint time)

 Cost: Hood, $750; hood grille, $65; hood pin kit, $95; paint, $300–$400

 Skill level: Hood installation: Easy; anyone can do it (painting must be left to a professional)

 Tools: No special tools required; drill, cutting wheel, or high-speed Dremel

One of the biggest body pieces on your Mustang is the hood. It's also one of the easiest to change, and it can make a big difference in the vehicle's overall appearance. There are obviously many hood styles available. Most are manufactured from fiberglass, and the quality of the construction, layers of fiberglass, and finished gel-coat are what differentiate a good hood from a bad one.

In cases like this, it's always good to go with a trusted manufacturer. Some will even offer the hood fully painted for an added cost. If your Mustang is new, this is one of the best options you could get. But if you've had your vehicle for a while, the sun can change the color of the original paint. You'll need to have a custom paint job to properly match the hood to the rest of the vehicle.

Nevertheless, installing an aftermarket hood is simple. The difficult part is aligning it and painting it. But a good body shop can also help you with that. In the case of the S197 Mustang, it's also a good idea to use a hood-pin kit to ensure

that the underhood pressures at highway speeds don't crack the hood or cause it to bulge or pop open.

In this application, we used a Shelby Performance CS6 hood, along with a billet hood pin kit No. 5R3Z-6316892-K. With the help of A-1 Auto Body in Escondido, California, the hood was also prepped and painted to a professional appearance.

SOURCES

A-1 Auto Body
825 North Andreason Dr. #C
Escondido, CA 92029
(760) 839-0404

Shelby Performance Parts LLC
130 Cassia Way
Henderson, NV 89014
(702) 405-3500
www.shelbyperformanceparts.com

This Shelby Performance Parts CS6 hood offers a sleek, performance appearance that gives a unique look to any Mustang GT. It's used on many Shelby vehicles, as well as the Shelby GT Hertz editions.

Our Mustang GT had the stock factory hood with nonfunctional hood scoop. This looks great, but we wanted the subtler yet more menacing appearance that the Shelby Performance Parts hood would provide.

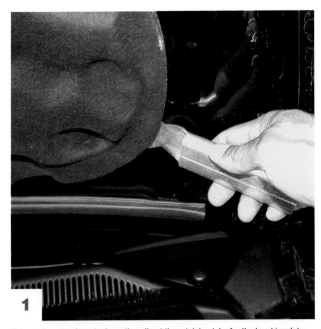

1

Using a door panel pry tool, gently pull out the retaining tabs for the hood insulator to access the hoses for the windshield washer nozzles.

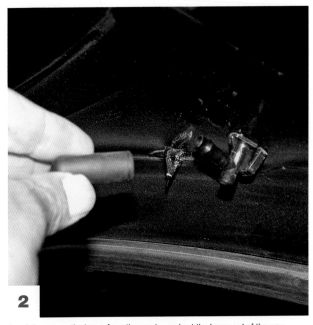

2

Carefully remove the hoses from the nozzles and set the hoses out of the way.

3

With some help holding the factory hood on the other side, you can remove the four bolts from the hood hinges. Make sure to store the hood in a location where it won't get scratched or damaged.

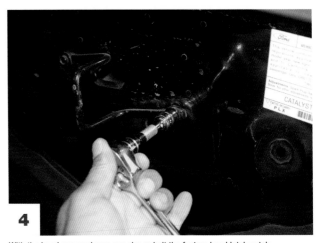

4

With the hood removed, you can also unbolt the factory hood latch catch.

5

With a friend holding the other side, simply bolt the Shelby Performance hood onto the car.

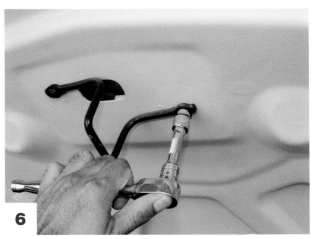

6

Then bolt the hood catch onto the Shelby Performance hood.

7

You can eyeball the alignment and adjust the rubber hood-stops to make sure the hood will close properly to deliver the vehicle over to A-1 Auto Body for prep and paint.

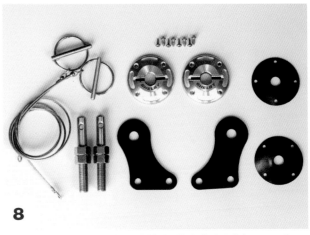

8

The Shelby Performance Parts hood-pin kit should also be installed to ensure the hood doesn't bulge at highway speeds. It comes with all of the necessary hardware and billet strike plates that will give the Mustang some added show detail.

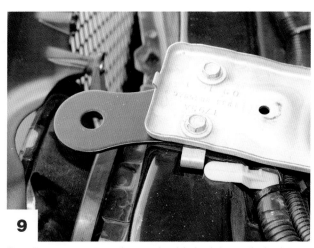

9 The radiator core support cover is removed, and the hood pin mounting brackets are bolted to the radiator core support braces.

10 From the underside of the radiator core support cover, mark the location of the hood-pin hole and drill through.

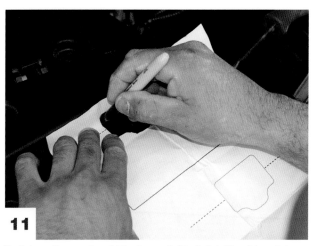

11 The hole provides a center point for placement of the included template so that you can mark where the cutouts need to be situated to properly fit the radiator core support cover over the hood-pin mounting brackets.

12 Here, you can see where we traced the outline of the template that marks where we need to cut.

13 A-1 Auto starts by using a cutting wheel and finishes removing the area with a high-speed Dremel tool to make as smooth a cut as possible.

14 The hood pin is then installed using one bolt on top and the other at the bottom to allow for height adjustment.

BODY AND EXTERIOR

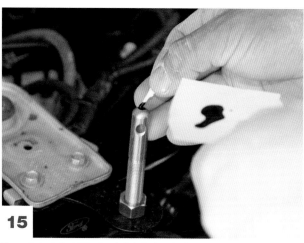

15

The next step is to drill the hood-pin holes into the hood. Use a dab of paint to gently close the hood and mark the location to drill. It's important to make sure that the hood is properly aligned at this point before drilling.

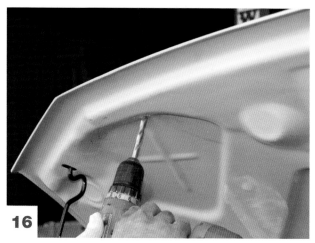

16

With the holes properly marked, the hood pins are drilled using a bit that is slightly smaller than the actual hood pins. This will allow you to widen the holes as necessary without taking off too much hood material.

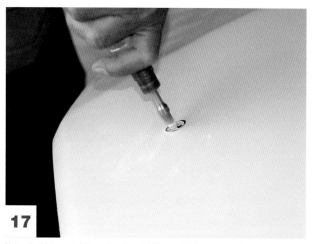

17

Using the high-speed Dremel tool or a high-speed drill, you can enlarge the holes and trial-fit the hood over the pins to see how much wider the holes need to be.

18

Here, you can see that after some widening, this hood pin still fit tight against the hood. Continue to widen the hole until there is a slight gap all around the pin.

19

With the hood pins drilled, A-1 Auto Body begins to prep the hood for paint. They use 320-grit sandpaper to take out any imperfections on the hood.

20

A-1 paints the underside first because it will allow better handling of the hood when adding some stripes and for final sanding and application of clearcoat for the top.

BODY AND EXTERIOR

158

21 Once the bottom is done, they paint the top of the hood and allow it to dry thoroughly before it will be wet-sanded, buffed, and clearcoated.

22 Because the hood can get damaged after it's been realigned, the hood's stripes and clearcoat are applied with the hood bolted and properly aligned on the car.

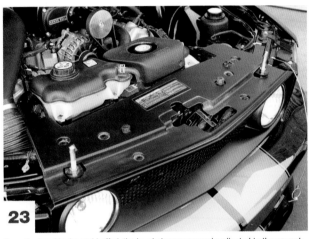

23 Once the hood is dry and buffed, the hood pins are properly adjusted to the correct height. The lanyards are also bolted to the radiator core support using the provided hardware, and the radiator core support is bolted in place.

24 The Shelby Performance Parts hood also uses this plastic grille that sits behind the inverted step in the hood. It's only ornamental, but it finishes off the appearance.

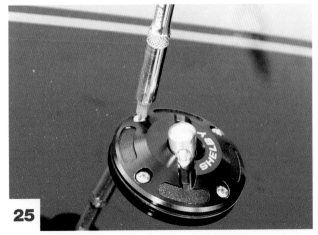

25 Finally, the plastic gasket and billet strike plate are bolted to the hood using the provided hardware. Shelby Performance Parts also sells black, hard-anodized billet strike plates that we installed instead of the natural billet pieces.

26 The finished installation with the Shelby Performance hood and hood-pin kit looks better than we could have ever anticipated. It gives a subtle yet menacing appearance to our Mustang GT that will last for many years.

BODY AND EXTERIOR

PROJECT 38
Installing a Performance Front Spoiler

 Agressive styling for your front end

 Time: 72 hours (includes prep, paint, and installation time)

Cost: $236 product (add $100 to $150 for paint)

 Skill level: Medium; some drilling, cutting, and knowledge of prepping ABS for paint are required

 Tools: No special tools; requires Sawzall or hacksaw blades and drill

While adding an aftermarket front spoiler or air-dam may only have a minimal effect on a car's ability to cut through the air, most of us install them to enhance the appearance of our Mustangs. Front spoilers and air-dams come in many styles and are manufactured from materials like ABS plastic, urethane, and fiberglass.

If you're going for a simple look, something like the factory GT-500 front spoiler, an ABS plastic spoiler is easy to install. But for those of us who want a more aggressive appearance, a urethane or fiberglass spoiler will typically give that type of look. They are more difficult to install, because they require prep and paint, so we sought help from A-1 Auto Body, a company that specializes in Mustang Shelby stripes,

hoods, and other accessories. As you can see, the end result dramatically changed the appearance of this Mustang GT.

SOURCES

Classic Design Concepts
42860 W. Nine Mile Rd.
Novi, MI 48375
(866) 624-7997
www.classicdesignconcepts.com

A-1 Auto Body
825 North Andreason Dr. #C
Escondido, CA 92029
(760) 839-0404

Classic Design Concepts makes this "aggressive" front chin spoiler that enhances the appearance of this Mustang GT by simply bolting on under the factory bumper. A-1 Auto Body prepped, painted, and demonstrated how to install the spoiler onto this Mustang GT.

BODY AND EXTERIOR

The CDC spoiler (No. 110021) is made from flexible urethane and comes unpainted. A-1 Auto Body recommends prepping the spoiler by sanding it with a fine 320-grit paper, then priming and painting it with a flex agent in the paint. This way, the spoiler can absorb minor bumps and dings without major damage.

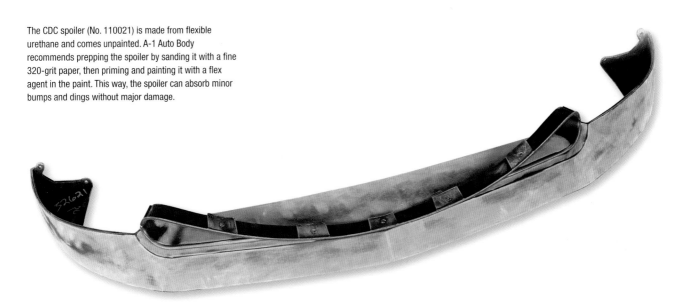

You'll have to remove the 5.5mm bolts to take off the factory slash shield from underneath the bumper. Then, from behind, you can access the locking tabs to remove this bumper grille. You can do this without taking off the bumper, but we did remove it because it made the cutting and paint prep easier for this installation, which was also getting some Shelby stripes.

After the grille is removed, follow the directions and cut off the grille mounting flanges, leaving the upper flanges in place. A-1 uses a hacksaw blade to make the cuts as carefully as possible.

The directions also call for cutting 1-inch back from the front surface of the factory fascia.

3

Here's a shot of the grille mounting flange that was cut out from the bumper.

4

Here, you can see the entire center section of the bumper lower grille opening cut out.

5

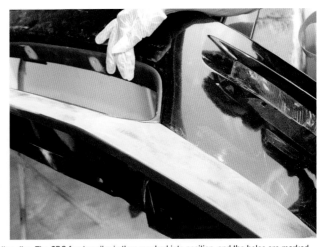

6

Cutting the factory bumper may leave some high spots, which A-1 removes with a sanding disc. The CDC front spoiler is then mocked into position, and the holes are marked to drill into the factory bumper.

A-1 finishes prepping and painting the spoiler. Once it is dry, the bonding agent and 3M tape are applied to the areas indicated in the instructions.

7

Button-head screws are used to secure the spoiler to the factory bumper. There's a large washer behind the screw that spreads the load across the top of this mounting area. As you can see, careful preparation and paint work are necessary to ensure that the stripes on this application line up correctly.

8

The front spoiler also attaches to the factory bumper at the edges, near the wheel wheels, to help secure it in place.

9

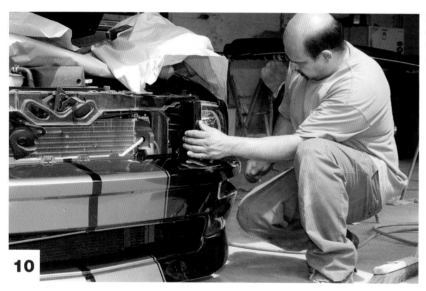

Before final assembly, attach the bumper and check the fit of the spoiler and its position. Then, remove the backing on the 3M adhesive and secure the button-head bolts, once you are sure everything lines up correctly.

10

Fully painted, striped, and installed, the spoiler looks like it's molded to the factory bumper.

11

PROJECT 39
GT to GT-500 Rear Spoiler Upgrade

 Spoiled rotten

 Time: 24 hours (includes prep, paint, and installation time)

 Cost: $229 product (add $80–100 for paint)

 Skill level: Easy once painted; anyone can do it

 Tools: No drilling required on GT with factory spoiler; no special tools

There are all types and styles of rear wings, but for die-hard Mustang fans, a sporty rear spoiler like that found on Shelby GT-500 and Roush cars is the best. The classic rear spoiler not only adds a dimension of speed and performance, but it's also more functional than the factory wing found on most GT-model Mustangs.

Fortunately, if your Mustang GT is equipped with a factory wing-style spoiler, the GT-500 spoiler is a direct bolt-in replacement. It's available through Ford Racing as part M16600SVTC and comes ready to be prepped and painted to match your vehicle.

SOURCE
A-1 Auto Body
825 North Andreason Dr. #C
Escondido, CA 92029
(760) 839-0404

The GT-500 rear spoiler is an easy swap for any Mustang GT equipped with a factory wing-style rear spoiler. You can get it through Ford Racing as a replacement or upgrade to your GT spoiler. Inset: The Ford Racing spoiler is made from ABS plastic and comes primed and ready for sanding and paint.

BODY AND EXTERIOR

To remove the factory wing-style spoiler, you simply open the trunk and remove the four bolts from the studs that secure the spoiler to the trunk lid.

The factory spoiler then simply lifts off the trunk lid.

Here, you can see the holes for the bolts that secure the factory spoiler in place. If your Mustang didn't come with a spoiler, you can measure and mark the studs on the Ford Racing spoiler and drill the holes through the trunk lid.

4

In this installation, our friends at A-1 Auto Body prepped and painted the Ford Racing spoiler to match the black paint and stripes they added to this Mustang GT. Here, they test-fit the spoiler after paint to ensure all the lines and bolt holes line up correctly.

5

Aside from the studs already mounted on the spoiler, the spoiler also has adhesive tape. Remove the backing prior to permanent installation on the trunk lid of your GT.

BODY AND EXTERIOR

6 A-1 places the spoiler into position and presses down so that the tape will adhere properly to the trunk lid. The bolts are then replaced on the other side of the trunk lid. Be careful not to over-tighten because it could damage the spoiler.

7 The finished result looks just like a Mustang GT-500 and only takes minutes to install. Most painters will need your fuel door to properly match the paint to your vehicle. A-1 Auto Body also primed, painted, wet-sanded, buffed, and polished our spoiler before it was installed.

PROJECT 40
Quarter Window Treatment

Some 1960s inspiration for a unique and modern upgrade

Time: 15 minutes

Cost: $89.95

Skill level: Easy; anyone can do it

Tools: No tools required; you will need isopropyl alcohol and a clean microfiber cloth

Because the S197 Mustangs were inspired by the design and shape of the 1960s models, many of the accessories on the classics also work well on their late-model cousins. One such case in point can be found in the rear quarter window accessories that can range from simple color-matching covers to louvers and complete window replacements.

The most popular are the louvers and covers that simply adhere over the factory windows. While color-matching styles are the norm, we decided to install a unique aluminum cover made by Shelby Performance Parts that is reminiscent of the vintage "R"-model race cars.

SOURCE

Shelby Performance Parts LLC
130 Cassia Way
Henderson, NV 89014
(702) 405-3500
www.shelbyperformanceparts.com

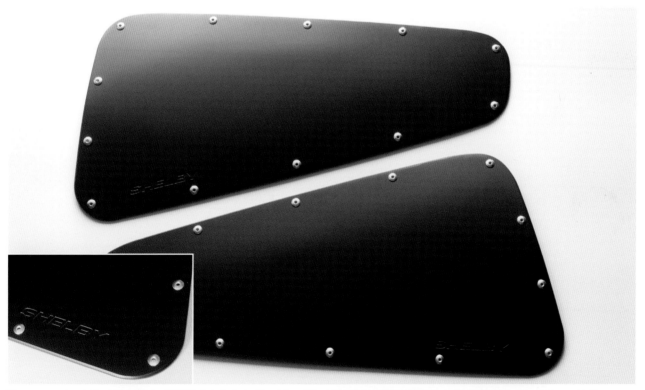

These rear quarter window covers give any S197 Mustang the look of the vintage "R"-model race cars that ran Trans-Am in the 1960s. Inset: The covers are made from lightweight aluminum and feature a black matte finish with simulated rivets and the Shelby logo stamped in the corner.

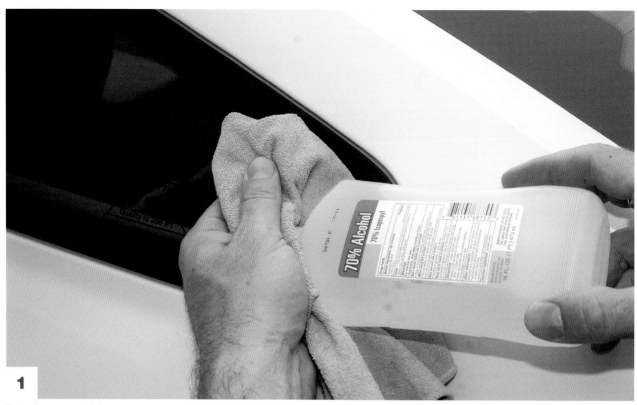

1

To install rear quarter window covers that adhere to the factory glass, you must first make sure it is clean and free of any oils or wax. We used isopropyl alcohol and a microfiber towel to thoroughly clean the window.

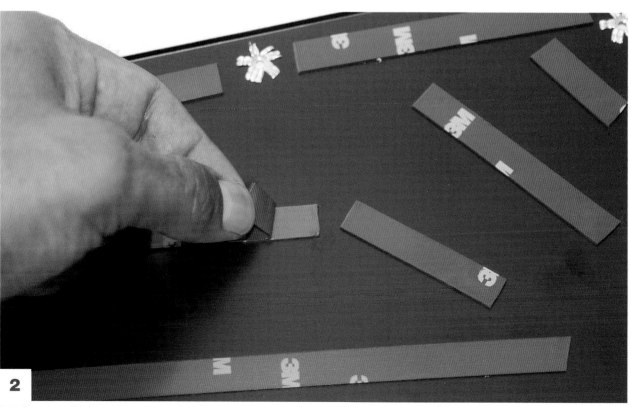

2

Behind the covers, 3M adhesive strips are strategically placed to secure the cover to the glass. Peel off the cover of each adhesive strip.

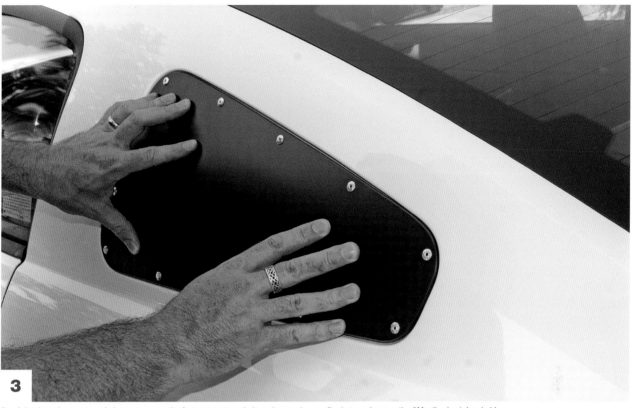

3 Carefully place the quarter window cover over the factory quarter window glass and press firmly to make sure the 3M adhesive takes hold.

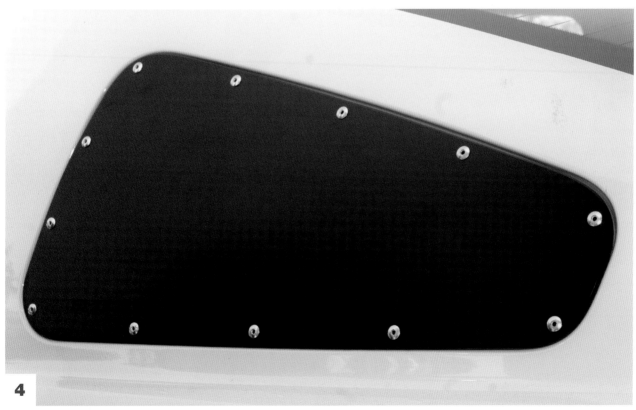

4 The finished look gives our S197 Mustang a vintage race appearance that stands out from louvers and color-matched covers.

PROJECT 41
Adding Sport Mirrors

 Reflect on your appearance

 Skill level: Easy; anyone can do it

 Time: 45 minutes

 Tools: Standard socket wrench set and Torx-bit screwdriver

S **Cost:** $219

A set of sportier mirrors is a subtle way of adding a racing-style appearance to your S197 Mustang. We installed on a 2007-model GT a set of Agent 47 mirrors that are based on the mirrors for the 1960s Mustangs and are more aerodynamic than the factory S197-model units. In addition, they simply bolt on and utilize the factory motors so that the mirror adjustments remain intact.

These mirrors are easy to install, but be aware that 2006-and-later Mustang models have an uncommon-looking harness for the mirror motor, with a saddle-style connection that has two clips on either side of the motor. It may require some thought to properly maneuver the harness out of the factory mirror shell.

SOURCE

Agent 47
2221 Rutherford Rd.
Carlsbad, CA 92008
(760) 496-3809
www.agentfourtyseven.com

BEFORE

AFTER

A sportier mirror inspired by those designed in the 1960s is more aerodynamic and can make your Mustang look even better.

Simply pry off the inside door panel section that covers the mirror bolts.

Disconnect the mirror motor wire harness and remove the three nuts holding the mirror in place.

The mirror glass is removed by pulling it toward you with a light tug.

Here you can see the clips behind the glass mirror that hold it in place on the motor.

Unbolt the motor using the correct Torx bit. Save the screws because they will be used to reinstall the motor into the Agent 47 mirror housing.

Remove the mirror studs, along with the weather-stripping foam, from the stock mirror.

Unplug the motor and thread the harness out from the mirror housing. Depending on the harness plug, you may have to maneuver it around to get it out.

7

Insert the harness into the new housing of the Agent 47 mirror.

8

Insert the motor and use the factory Torx screws to secure it to the new housing.

9

BODY AND EXTERIOR

175

10

Install the supplied mirrors onto the motors by pushing down so that the clips snap in place.

11

Screw the original mirror studs into the Agent 47 mirror housing and reinsert the mirror with the weather-stripping back onto the door.

BODY AND EXTERIOR

12 Plug the wiring harness back together and bolt the mirror into its original position using the factory nuts.

13 Reinstall the plastic cover above the door panel, and the installation is complete.

PROJECT 42
Grille Upgrade

 Customizing the front end

 Time: 1 hour

 Cost: $359

 Skill level: Easy; bolt-on with mild modifications

 Tools: No special tools; requires flathead and Phillips screwdrivers, drill with ¼-inch bit

Changing out the grille on your Mustang is a quick and easy way to give it a unique look. Aftermarket grilles come in a variety of designs, materials, and finishes, so you can pick one to fit the look of your car. You can also choose to retain the auxiliary lights, move them to the center, or delete them completely, depending on the grille you purchase. Also, if you'd rather not completely replace the grille, many companies offer an insert or an overlay that fits over the stock grille so that you can remove it easily at any time.

Agent 47 in Carlsbad, California, offers a unique grille replacement that is constructed of a high-quality plastic frame and a metal mesh center section with an optional logo. The recessed opening creates a longer hood overhang for a more retro look, and the mesh also helps to increase airflow to the radiator. The entire assembly clips into the factory holes, and the fog lights, although moved slightly more to the outside, fit directly into the new grille.

The installation is relatively simple and only requires small modifications. Removing the grille requires you to unbolt the radiator cover, unplug the wiring harnesses from the lights, and release the tabs that hold the grille in place. To make the lights fit into the new grille, two tabs on the lights need be trimmed down, and new holes need to be drilled, but overall the installation should take less than an hour.

SOURCE

Agent 47
2221 Rutherford Road
Carlsbad, CA 92008
(760) 496-3809
www.agentfortyseven.com

The stock grille on the Mustang GT is made of hard plastic and features a honeycomb design with pony emblem in the middle and auxiliary lights mounted at each end. Above: Here you see the Agent 47 product with an inner metal mesh grille and the light housings pushed farther to the outside. The mesh allows additional air to reach the radiator and helps to keep it cool.

1

The first step is to remove the plastic radiator cover by pulling up on the fasteners that hold it down. Keep the fasteners for later because you will reuse them.

2

With the fasteners removed, pull up on the radiator cover to remove it and set it aside.

3

Agent 47 recommends putting tape down on the front bumper to prevent scratches and dings when removing and installing the grille

4

With the radiator cover removed, you will see the wiring harnesses that connect to the lights in the grille. You will need to unplug both before you remove the grille.

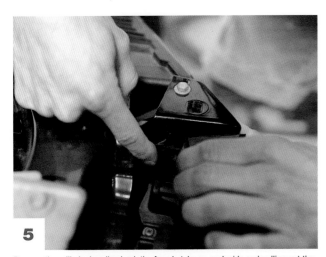

5

Remove the grille by bending back the female tabs on each side and pulling out the male ends.

6

With the lights disconnected and the tabs released, pull the grille away from the car.

BODY AND EXTERIOR

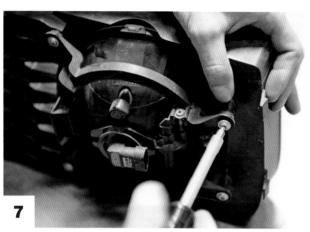

7

The lights need to be transferred from the old grille to the new grille. Take them out by removing the four screws on the tabs that secure the light to the grille.

8

With the screws removed, take out the lights and align the two inner holes with those on the Agent 47 grille.

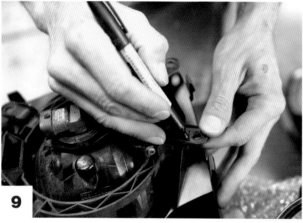

9

The holes in the two outer tabs will not line up with those on the grille and will need to be modified. In addition, portions of those tabs will need to be removed for clearance. With a marker, draw a line across each tab just inside the hole that is parallel to the side of the grille.

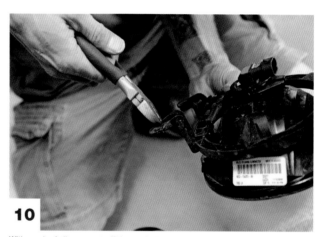

10

With a pair of clippers, cut off the marked part of each tab.

11

Fit the light back onto the Agent 47 grille and find where the hole lines up with the remaining portion of the tab. Mark the spot and, using a ¼-inch drill, cut a new hole that lines up with the one on the grille. If you need to, you can start by using a smaller bit size and file the remaining portion of the hole.

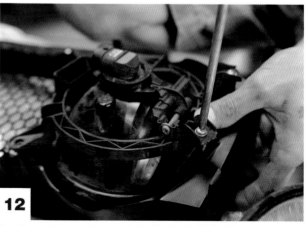

12

Once the new holes have been created on the tabs, install the lights into the Agent 47 grille using the supplied screws. Do not reuse the factory screws.

BODY AND EXTERIOR

13

Here, you can see the Agent 47 grille with the lights installed compared to the stock grille.

14

Install the Agent 47 grille by reinserting the male ends on the grille into the female tabs on the car and pushing it into place.

15

Reconnect the wiring harnesses for each of the lights.

16

Put the plastic radiator cover back in place, and secure it using the original fasteners.

With the radiator cover in place, remove the tape on the bumper. The installation is finished.

17

PROJECT 43
Sequential Taillight Upgrade

 Sending the right signals

Time: 30 minutes

Cost: $156

Skill level: Easy; anyone can do it

 Tools: No special tools required; you'll need an 11mm open-end wrench or long socket and a small screwdriver

There are several unique accessories that add custom detail to your S197 Mustang. Among these are sequential taillights that turn each of the three rear taillight bulbs on in sequence as you make a right or left turn and when you come to a stop. Classic Design Concepts manufactures a kit that's easy to install by simply replacing the factory rear taillight wiring harness. This kit gives your Mustang a custom function that will get your vehicle noticed.

SOURCE

Classic Design Concepts LLC
42860 W. Nine Mile Rd.
Novi, MI 48375
(866) 624-7997
www.classicdesignconcepts.com

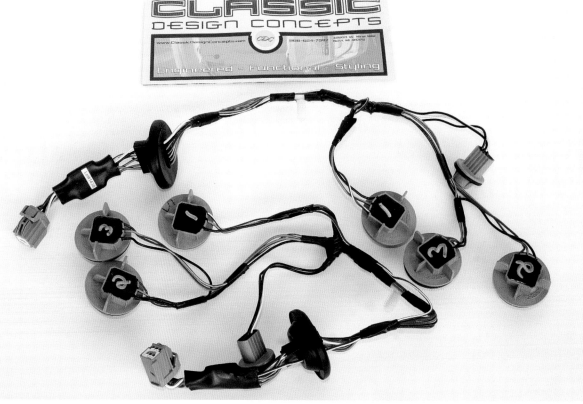

The CDC sequential taillight wiring harness has built-in electronics that provide the lighting sequence for each of the three taillight bulbs.

BODY AND EXTERIOR

Start by opening the trunk and removing the three plastic pop-rivets with a small screwdriver. There are also two plastic wing nuts that are attached to the taillight studs that must also be removed.

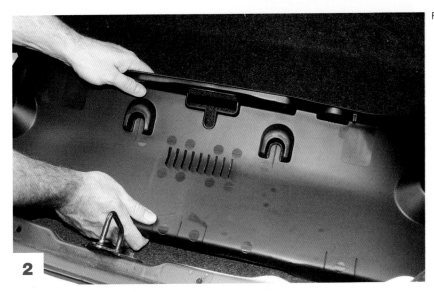

Remove the plastic trunk panel and place it out of the way.

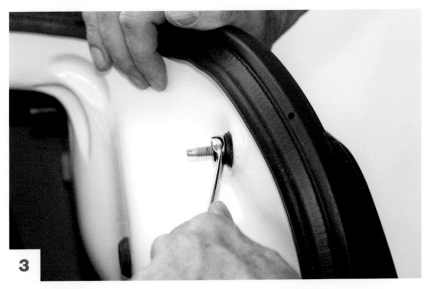

Use an 11mm wrench or a long socket ratcheting wrench to remove the three bolts from the taillight studs.

With the bolts removed, the taillight housing can be pulled away from the body.

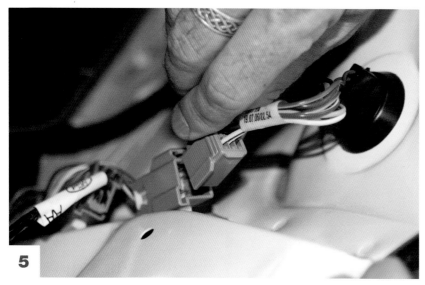

Unplug the wiring harness from the inside of the trunk area and push it through the factory hole in the trunk.

Twist each bulb socket so that it unlocks from the taillight housing.

Remove each bulb by pulling it up out of the socket, then replace each bulb into the CDC wiring harness.

The CDC harness is numbered so that the No. 1 socket goes into the outer light bar (closest to the fender). Plug in the rest of the sockets in sequence, including the reverse light socket and bulb.

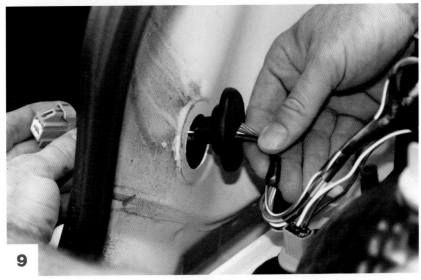

While holding the taillight in place, reroute the new wiring harness through the trunk sheet metal and secure the grommet.

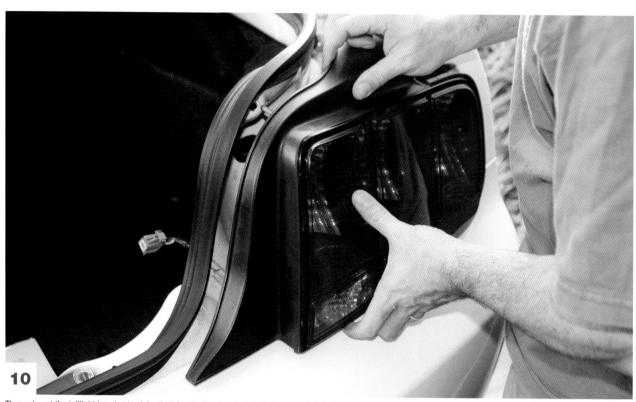

10 Then reinsert the taillight housing back in place by aligning the studs to their appropriate holes.

11 Reinstall the bolts. Some silicone is used to prevent vibration noises. Make sure you reuse the silicone on each stud. Do not over-tighten. Then check the lights to make sure they are in working order before reattaching the plastic trunk panel. All three lights should light up when the brake is depressed. When the turn signal is activated, each light will light up in sequence, indicating the direction of travel.

PROJECT 44
Installing a Rear Deck Lid Trim Panel

 A total blackout

 Time: 15 minutes

Cost: $160

Skill level: Easy; anyone can do it

Tools: No special tools required; you'll need masking or painter's tape, a plastic or wood wedge, a heat gun or hair dryer, isopropyl alcohol, and a microfiber cloth

I f you're one of those Mustang enthusiasts who like the look of the classic 1960s and 1970s models with a flat-black rear deck lid, a better way to do this (instead of using paint) is with a trim panel. We selected the Classic Design Concepts rear deck lid trim panel that is made from UV-stable ABS plastic. It adds a louvered design that really gives a custom look to the S197 Mustang.

SOURCE
Classic Design Concepts LLC
42860 W. Nine Mile Rd.
Novi, MI 48375
866-624-7997
www.classicdesignconcepts.com

Adding a deck lid trim panel gives a late-model S197 Mustang the look of the classic 1960s and 1970s models.

The CDC deck lid trim panel is made from UV-resistant ABS plastic and fills the deep recess of the deck lid to make the modification look much better than flat paint.

1 Using some masking or painter's tape to protect the vehicle's finish, pry the chrome factory medallion off using a door-pry tool. You can also use a plastic or wood wedge if you're afraid of scratching the paint.

2 Because our vehicle was new, the adhesive from the medallion didn't leave lots of residue. Nevertheless, you'll need isopropyl alcohol and a clean cloth, preferably a microfiber cloth, to remove any residue. If you have lots or residue left, you can use a heat gun or hair dryer to heat up the adhesive, as long as you don't overheat the paint.

3

Remove small 2-inch sections of the adhesive tape at the rear of the deck lid panel. This will allow you to center the panel and make minor adjustments.

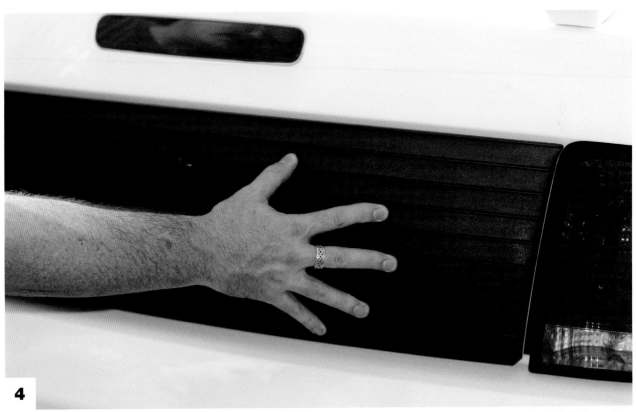

4

Center the panel onto the deck lid and pull the adhesive backside out from underneath. Then apply pressure to the panel to seat the adhesive, and the installation is complete.

PROJECT 45
Adding a Custom Fuel Door

 A performance look is in the details

 Time: 30 minutes

Cost: $150 (product)

 Skill level: Easy; can be done by beginner or novice

 Tools: No special tools; requires 7mm open-end wrench and ⁵⁄₁₆ open-end wrench

Small details add up when you want to give your Mustang a custom or performance look. Items like a billet fuel door always add to the performance appeal of any vehicle, and they are very easy to install. Custom fuel doors vary in price, style, manufacturing materials, and finishes, such as brushed aluminum, chrome, paint, or powder coat. You can also have them painted to match the color of your Mustang, which is a popular modification. Whatever you choose, keep in mind that the doors will always be exposed to the elements, so make sure that the materials and finish you select will survive the elements, and your fuel door will look great for years to come.

Installing a custom fuel door is simple, no matter which style you choose. In this instance, we wanted to add a subtle look to a black Mustang GT, so we added the Shelby Performance Parts billet fuel door No. 5S3Z-66405A26BK. The door has a matte-black, E-coat finish that looks awesome against the black finish of the GT and will look good for a long time.

SOURCE

Shelby Performance Parts LLC
130 Cassia Way
Henderson, NV 89014
(702) 405-3500
www.shelbyperformanceparts.com

This Shelby Performance billet fuel door features a black, E-anodized finish that looks great against a solid-black GT or GT-500.

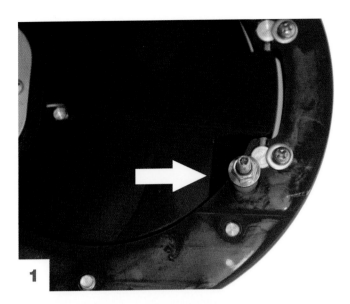

The billet fuel door uses three studs. Each has two spacers to sandwich between the factory fuel door flange and the retaining bolts.

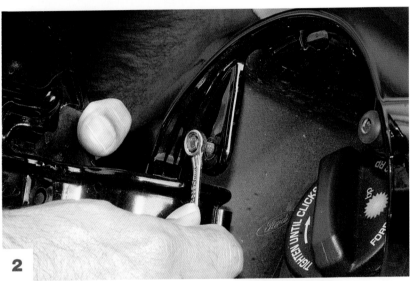

To remove the factory door, you'll need a 7mm wrench to take off both bolts that hold it in place. Pry out the fuel cap retaining strap from the door with a set of long-nose pliers or a large flathead screwdriver.

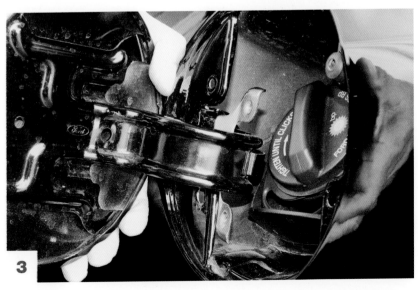

Gently remove the fuel door from the fender, making sure not to scratch the paint. Leave the factory fuel cap in place to prevent gasoline fumes from escaping. You will also have to remove the bottom-right rubber doorstop.

BODY AND EXTERIOR

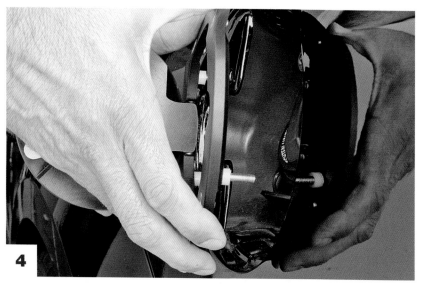

With one plastic spacer on each stud, insert the billet fuel door into the holes in the fender and secure them with the bolts provided. Tighten them until snug using a $\frac{5}{16}$ open-end wrench.

4

We secured the fuel cap strap onto the bottom-left stud, which added some space to make the billet fuel door fit flush onto the fender.

5

The finished installation looks great. The black anodized door gives this GT a subtle performance look that will last for many years.

6

BODY AND EXTERIOR

SECTION 6
INTERIOR

PROJECT 46
Adding Billet Door Trim

 Easy ways to upgrade the look of your interior

 Skill level: Easy

 Time: 1 hour (install all pieces)

 Tools: T20 Torx-head wrench, SAE and metric socket set, Phillips and flathead screwdrivers, door handle clip tool

$ Cost: Seat recliner levers, $69.95; sill plate accent bars, $29.95; cup holder trim, $59.95; door lock grommet covers, $14.95; billet coat hooks, $19.95; shoulder belt mount accents, $24.95; lumbar switch cover, $7.95; seat adjust switch cover, $7.95

Adding highlights to your Mustang's interior can be as simple as applying some billet trim pieces and covers. Most are very easy to install because they use adhesive tape to fit over existing plastic pieces. There are many covers and trim pieces available, so we decided to gather some of the more popular pieces manufactured by Scott Drake Enterprises, and sold through Shelby Performance Parts, to add some flash to this Mustang's dull interior.

The pieces we selected will accent our seat adjustment controls, center console, door, and interior trim. There are many more pieces available, but the installation is typically the same. Many of these pieces use an adhesive that sticks to the factory plastic, so it will need to be cleaned thoroughly with isopropyl alcohol and a clean cloth.

SOURCE

Shelby Performance Parts LLC
130 Cassia Way
Henderson, NV 89014
(702) 405-3500
www.shelbyperformanceparts.com

Billet accent pieces brighten up your Mustang's interior. Here, we used some Scott Drake pieces that are easy to install and can be mixed and matched to your own taste.

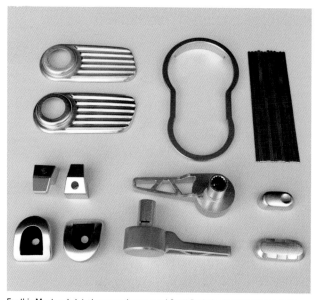

For this Mustang's interior upgrade, we used Scott Drake's shoulder belt accents, lumbar and seat adjustment covers, seat recliner levers, coat hooks, cup holder trim, door lock grommet covers, and sill plate accents.

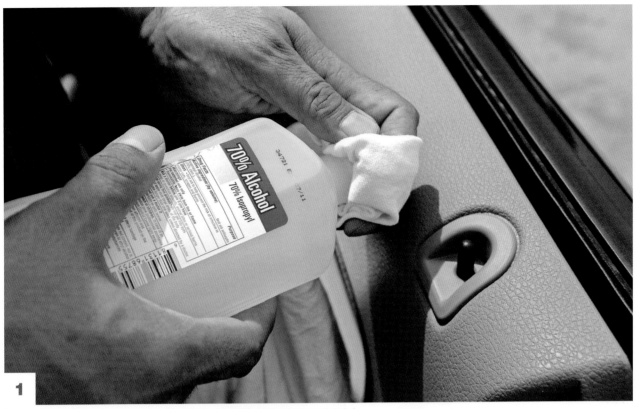

Start with the installation of door lock grommet covers by cleaning the area with isopropyl alcohol.

Next, peel back the cover to expose the adhesive tape.

Apply firm and even pressure to ensure the tape gets a hold on the plastic.

3

The finished grommet cover looks great and provides some much-needed detail to this door panel.

4

Again, clean the door sill plate with alcohol and a clean cloth.

5

INTERIOR

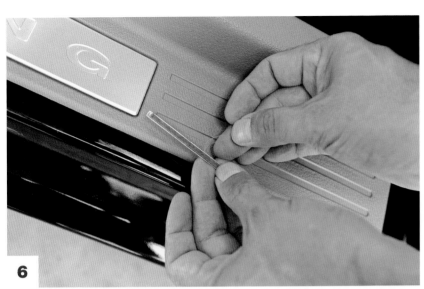

Each door sill accent comes with an adhesive tape from which you need to remove the backing.

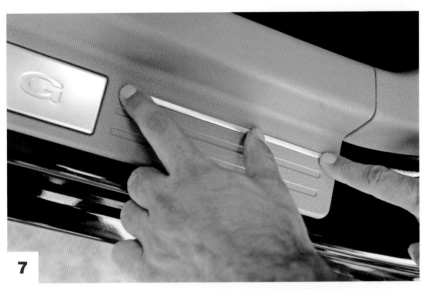

Firmly press down on the billet piece to make sure the adhesive sticks.

The finished sill plate looks pretty cool with these billet accents added to it.

INTERIOR

197

PROJECT 47
Adding Interior Billet Pieces

 Easy ways to upgrade the look of your interior

 Time: 1 hour (install all pieces)

Cost: Seat recliner levers, $69.95; sill plate accent bars, $29.95; cup holder trim, $59.95; door lock grommet covers, $14.95; billet coat hooks, $19.95; shoulder belt mount accents, $24.95; lumbar switch cover, $7.95; seat adjust switch cover, $7.95

 Skill level: Easy

 Tools: T20 Torx-head wrench, SAE and metric socket set, Phillips and flathead screwdrivers, door handle clip tool

SOURCE

Shelby Performance Parts LLC
130 Cassia Way
Henderson, NV 89014
(702) 405-3500
www.shelbyperformanceparts.com

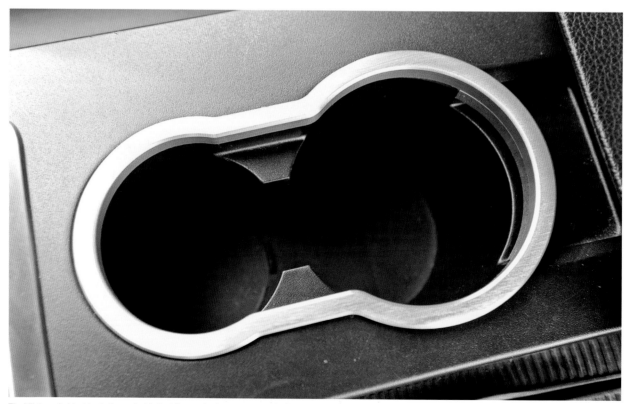

The billet cup holder trim is the easiest to install, you simply press it into place so that it fits snug over the factory plastic console.

INTERIOR

198

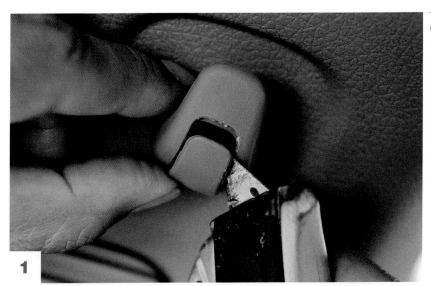

The coat hooks require you to release the center cover with a thin screwdriver or box cutter.

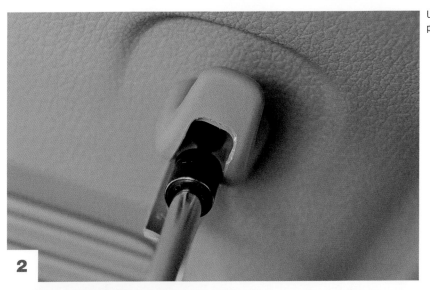

Use a Torx-20 bit to remove the screw that holds the plastic coat hook in place.

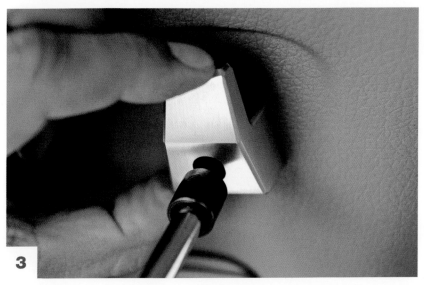

Screw in the new billet coat hook using the factory Torx-head screw.

INTERIOR

PROJECT 48
Adding Billet Seat Accents

 Easy ways to upgrade the look of your interior

Time: 1 hour (install all pieces)

 Cost: Seat recliner levers, $69.95; sill plate accent bars, $29.95; cup holder trim, $59.95; door lock grommet covers, $14.95; billet coat hooks, $19.95; shoulder belt mount accents, $24.95; lumbar switch cover, $7.95; seat adjust switch cover, $7.95

Skill level: Easy

Tools: T20 Torx-head wrench, SAE and metric socket set, Phillips and flathead screwdrivers, door handle clip tool

SOURCE

Shelby Performance Parts LLC
130 Cassia Way
Henderson, NV 89014
(702) 405-3500
www.shelbyperformanceparts.com

1 Installation of the shoulder belt accents requires temporary removal of the belt. You accomplish this by first prying open the bolt cover with a small screwdriver.

2 Unbolt the seat belt from the door pillar using a socket wrench.

Clean the accent area with alcohol to ensure the adhesive sticks.

Peel back the adhesive covers on the back of the accent.

Apply even pressure and make sure the piece is in proper position.

INTERIOR

6 Replace the shoulder belt, and you can see these minor accents make a big difference.

7 Removal of the seat lever is a little more difficult. You will need a door handle clip removal tool.

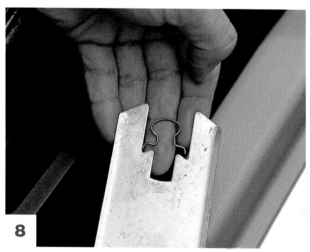

8 Gently push the tool in from the back of the handle to remove the clip.

9 It may take several tries, but once the clip is removed, you can pull out the factory handle.

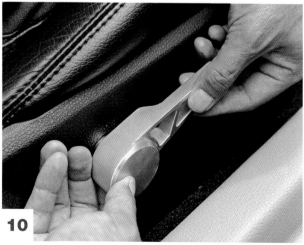

10 The Scott Drake billet handle pushes into place.

11 Use the clip tool to gently push the clip back into position.

12

The seat adjuster button is also cleaned with alcohol to remove any dirt or oil.

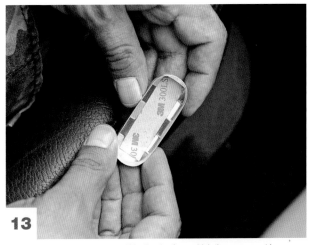

13

The adjuster button cover uses a 3M adhesive from which the cover must be peeled back.

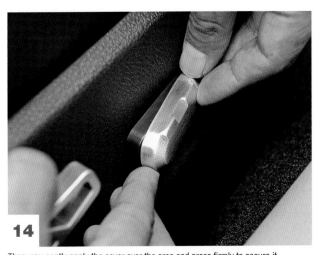

14

Then, you gently apply the cover over the area and press firmly to secure it into place.

15

Our finished passenger seat looks great with its billet handle and adjuster.

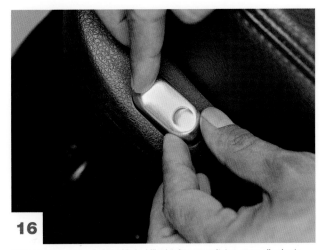

16

On the driver's side, we also added a billet lumbar cover. It, too, uses adhesive to hold it in place.

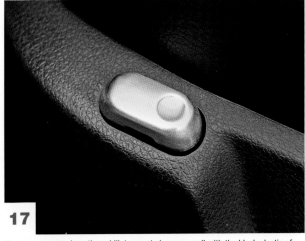

17

Here, you can see how these billet accent pieces go well with the black plastic of this Mustang's interior.

PROJECT 49
Custom Arm Rest Cover

 Customize your interior with a new arm rest cover

 Time: 1 hour

Cost: $40

 Skill level: Medium; requires some upholstery knowledge

 Tools: upholstery scissors, upholstery glue

Custom embroidery on interior pieces instantly shows that your interior is unique. But you don't have to have all your upholstery upgraded to have the same effect. Your Mustang's arm rest can be easily upgraded with an embroidered piece that can customize your interior at a fraction of the cost.

You'll need some upholstery experience to know how to trim and apply this cover to your center console. It's best to practice on some old interior pieces first if you're doing this for the first time.

SOURCE

Shelby Performance Parts LLC
130 Cassia Way
Henderson, NV 89014
(702) 405-3500
www.shelbyperformanceparts.com

INTERIOR

BEFORE

After

This custom-embroidered arm rest cover looks great and is easy to install if you have a little bit of upholstery experience. Inset: The factory arm rest cover doesn't grab your attention like one with a big *GT Mustang* embroidered across the top of it.

We found this inexpensive cover, manufactured by Scott Drake and sold through Shelby Performance Parts, that matches our Mustang's custom look.

1

Begin by removing the four screws that hold the arm rest lid in place.

INTERIOR

With the four screws out, you can remove the arm rest from the center console.

Remove the six Phillips-head screws from the arm rest inner lid.

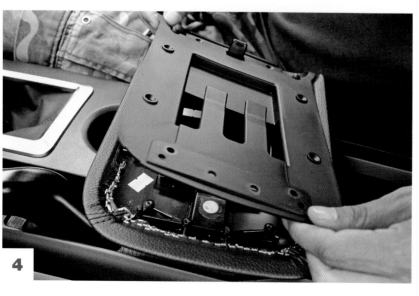

Remove the lid, and you'll see how the factory cover is glued and stapled to the arm rest shell.

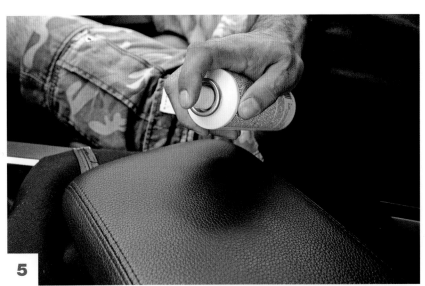

Use an upholstery spray adhesive over the entire area of the factory arm rest.

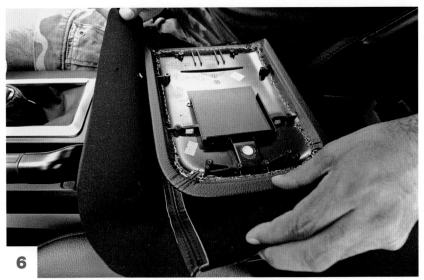

Make sure the embroidery is in the correct position, and start folding the new piece over the factory arm rest.

The edges are where your upholstery techniques come into play. You can fold the edges over tightly and trim the rest using upholstery scissors. Then glue it down for a smooth finish.

INTERIOR

PROJECT 50
Installing an Aftermarket Fuel Pressure Gauge

 It's good to be properly informed

 Time: 4–6 hours

$ **Cost:** Fuel pressure gauge, $200 (No. 4963); Speed of Sound dual-gauge pillar pod, $120; wiring connectors, extra 18-gauge wire, and Add-a-Circuit, $15–20.

 Skill level: Medium; requires some knowledge of wiring

 Tools: Wiring strippers, wiring crimpers, wire cutters, SAE standard and metric wrenches, 12-volt wiring probe

Gauges typically do more than give your Mustang's interior a race-inspired look. The right gauges can identify problems with your engine and help you monitor its performance. Because many Mustang owners supercharge their vehicles, we decided to add two of the most important gauges for this application. These include a boost and a fuel pressure gauge.

The biggest problem with installing gauges is to find the right 12-volt ignition source. We found an unused fuse connection on the fuse box, located on the passenger-side kick panel. This is the best place to get a reliable 12-volt ignition source with a fuseable link, when used with an Add-a-Circuit.

It's also important to note that a negative wire is located under the dash to the right of the steering column, closest to the center console. You can attach your ground wires here if you are mounting your gauges on the driver's-side pillar mount. For gauges mounted at the center of the dashboard, you can also use an existing negative wire located just behind the glove box.

Make sure all your wiring is neat and clean and that your wires are organized, zip-tied, and out of the way of the driver's foot, brake and clutch pedals, and other areas that may cause the wires to become accidentally pulled or cut.

It's also a good idea to test your connections with the gauges attached before you place them into your gauge pods. This way you can check any improper connections and enjoy your gauges once they are finally installed.

SOURCES

Speed of Sound LLC
(866) 48-GAUGE
www.speedofsoundllc.com

Autometer Products Inc.
413 West Elm Street
Sycamore, IL 60178
(866) 248-6356
www.autometer.com

Kenne Bell Superchargers
10743 Bell Court
Rancho Cucamonga, CA 91730
(909) 941-6646
www.kennebell.net

Two of the most crucial gauges you need for your supercharged Mustang are a boost gauge and a fuel pressure gauge. These are easy to install with a few helpful tips.

1 For our installation, we started by using an Autometer Ultra-Lite II fuel pressure gauge (No. 4963). It's an electric, 2¹⁄₁₆-inch gauge with full sweep that's easy to install and is very accurate.

2 The gauge comes with a wiring harness and electrical pressure sender that will attach to your factory fuel rail.

3 As part of the preparation, search for where you can attach the gauge's light source to your Mustang's interior lights. Using a small screwdriver, gently pull out the light switch from the dash.

4 Some Ford techs told us that the yellow wire with a blue stripe was the interior 12-volt light wire that would be perfect for our gauges. We checked it with a probe and found it was indeed the correct wire for our 2007 model.

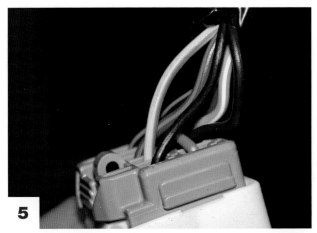

5 Other models may have a different color wire, but the correct one should be in the same location on the light switch harness. Because you'll be mounting the gauges in a driver's-side pillar pod, this is a perfect spot.

6 The factory fuel rail has a Schrader valve that's used to connect a fuel pressure gauge tester. This will be removed to attach the Autometer sending unit.

INTERIOR

7

Because the sending unit is a ⅛ NPT fitting, you need an adaptor to connect it to the factory fuel metering block. We used this adaptor from Kenne Bell, but you can also get one from your local parts store for less than three dollars.

8

Make sure the engine is completely cold so there is no pressure in the fuel line when removing the Schrader valve and installing the sender and adaptors. You should also use Teflon tape to ensure a tight fit. Don't over-tighten the fittings because they are going into an aluminum fuel block.

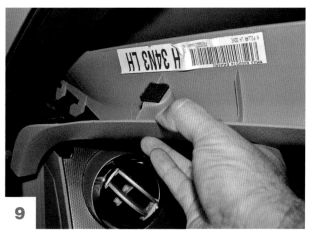

9

Move back into the interior and pull away the factory door pillar molding. The front piece must be unhooked from the dash by pulling it back and away.

10

For our application, we used a Speed of Sound dual-gauge pillar pod in Dove Gray.

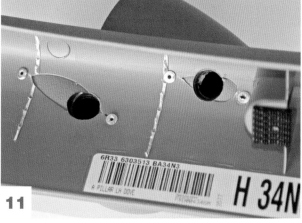

11

The Speed of Sound pods are built into a factory pillar molding and have access holes to route the wiring and tubing through to the gauges.

12

Route the wiring from the engine down to the firewall, where a harness opening is visible. You will find this large harness grommet that had a small indentation in it. Cut a small hole and route the wires through to the dash.

INTERIOR

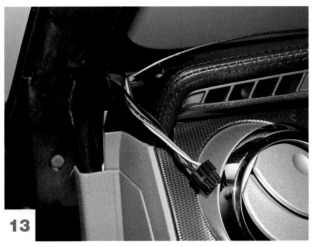

13

From under the dash, zip-tie the harness and route it up through to the pillar area.

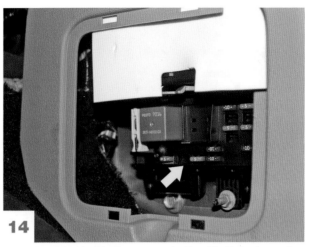

14

You will also need a 12-volt ignition-on source. Looking at the Mustang's manual, we found the fuse box on the passenger side of the vehicle and located an unused fuse port between the two 5-amp fuses.

15

At the auto parts store, you should purchased an Add-a-Circuit and connect it to the port.

16

This gives you a 12-volt ignition-on circuit to power your fuel pressure gauge. Because the boost gauge is mechanical, it only needs a negative and a 12-volt interior light source.

Use a round file to make a hole in the fuse box cover to accommodate your 12-volt wire, which is routed along the existing harness to the driver's side of the dash.

17

Slip all the wiring and tubing through the Speed of Sound pillar mount and connect everything to the gauges, making sure there's plenty of wire slack hanging from under the dash. Once it is in place, snap the pillar gauge pod into the factory position.

18

The Autometer 2 1/16-inch gauges fit snug into the Speed of Sound pods and don't require any glue or bolts to hold them in place.

19

The fuel pressure gauge will also indicate any problems in the fuel delivery, including clogged injectors, a tired fuel pump, and more.

20

INTERIOR

PROJECT 51
Installing an Aftermarket Boost Gauge

? **It's good to be properly informed**

Time: 4–6 hours

$ **Cost:** Boost gauge, $80 (No. 4907)

★ **Skill level:** Medium; requires some knowledge of wiring

Tools: Wiring strippers, wiring crimpers, wire cutters, SAE standard and metric wrenches, 12-volt wiring probe

1 At this point it is time to start setting up your boost gauge. Use an Autometer vacuum/boost mechanical gauge (No. 4907).

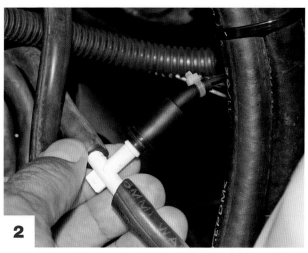

2 The gauge comes with clear plastic tubing and a T-fitting to tap into the boost line. In our case, the boost line was larger than the supplied T-fitting, so we had to get a larger T-fitting from the auto parts store. Here, you can see the boost line attached to the Kenne Bell supercharger's boost line.

The boost line is routed through the firewall in the same manner as the fuel pressure wiring, and the compression fitting is added to the other end. You can use a wire hangar to pull the boost line through. Just be sure not to kink the line, or it can break.

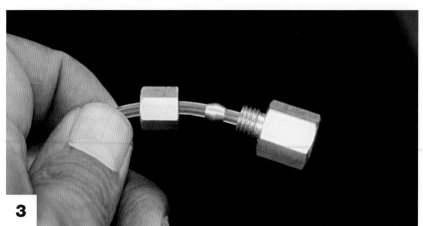

3

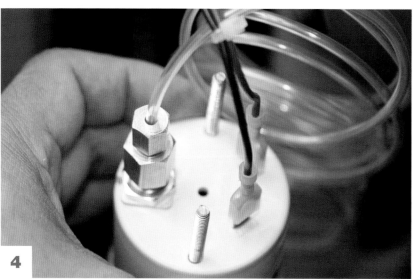

Pull the boost line through the dash area near the pillar mount and connect the fitting to the gauge. You should also connect a 12-volt lead and negative ground lead to the boost gauge's terminals.

4

Next, connect your wiring. The beige wire is the 12-volt lighting wire on the fuel gauge harness, while the red wire connects to the 12-volt lighting terminal on the back of the boost gauge. The negative ground wires are attached to an existing ground wire found on the dash frame, located to the right of the steering column under the dash. The 12-volt ignition-on wire is attached to the wiring harness of the fuel pressure gauge.

5

With all the wires neatly zip-tied together and tucked away so they do not interfere with the clutch pedal or other areas, you can enjoy your gauges. The boost gauge will tell you how much boost the Kenne Bell supercharger is making. Any variation in boost or vacuum levels can indicate potential problems with the system.

6

PROJECT 52
Installing a Roll Cage

 Rage in the cage

 Time: 5–6 hours

Cost: $509.95

Skill level: Medium; some drilling and modifications required

Tools: No special tools; requires electric drill with ¼-inch bit and razor blade or X-Acto knife

If you plan to use your 2005-and-later Mustang as a weekend racer at the drag strip or on a road course, then it is good to consider installing a roll bar or cage. In fact, the NHRA requires a roll bar for any convertible running 13.49 seconds or quicker in the quarter mile and in any other car at 11.49 seconds. A full roll cage is required in any vehicle running 9.99 seconds or quicker or with a trap speed of 135 miles per hour or more.

Autopower Industries in San Diego, California, has been manufacturing racing equipment for over 35 years and offers a variety of roll bars and cages that are designed to fit each individual application. The roll bar installed in this Mustang is Autopower's street-sport version that is constructed from 1.75-inch mild steel tubing with four mounting points. It also features a bolt-in harness mount tube that can be removed for easy access to the rear seats. Both street and race roll bars are also available, as well as bolt-in and welded roll cages.

The installation is simple, although a second person is needed to keep the roll bar in place while holes are being drilled at the mounting points. The interior needs to be stripped down to the metal, including the front and rear seats and carpet, to allow the bar to be bolted to the car at the rear wheelwell and on the floor in front of the rear seats. Some modification must also be done to the interior trim and carpet to allow the roll bar to pass through. Overall, allow 5–6 hours for the installation.

SOURCE
Autopower Industries
3424 Pickett St.
San Diego, CA 92110
(619) 297-3300
www.autopowerindustries.com

Autopower Industries hand-builds custom roll bars and cages specific for each car, ensuring that each one fits precisely for every application.

INTERIOR

1 Before the roll bar can be installed, much of the interior needs to be removed. We recommend starting at the rear and moving forward. Here, you can see the rear seats have been completely removed.

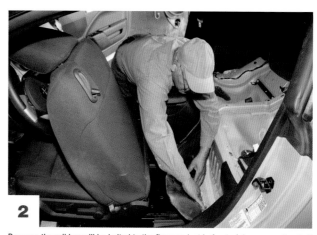

2 Because the roll bar will be bolted to the floorpan just in front of the rear seats, all of the carpeting in that area needs to be pulled up.

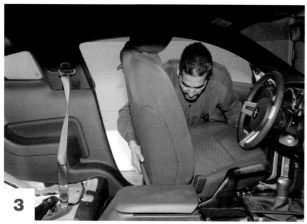

3 The Autopower roll bar could technically be installed with the front seats in place, but it makes it a lot easier to remove them.

4 With the interior stripped down to the metal, the roll bar can be placed inside the car. It helps to have two people during this stage of the installation to keep all the mounting points in place for the best possible fitment.

5 The rear mounting point is on the inside of the wheelwell and should fit just inside the sound-deadening material.

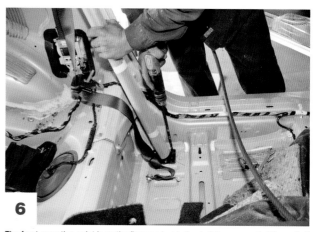

6 The front mounting point is on the floorpan just in front of the rear seats. When all of the mounting points fit snugly, it is time to drill the holes for the bolts that will hold the bar in place. It is important to have someone hold the bar in place while drilling so that it does not shift or move.

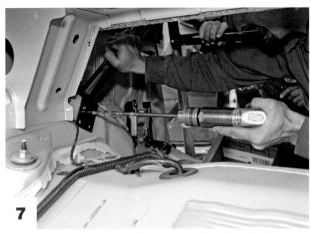

7

Here, you can see the holes being drilled for the mounting point on the left rear wheelwell. Once the holes have been drilled, insert the included bolts to help keep the bar in place.

8

The mounting points will also be secured from outside the car. Here, you can see one of the plates inside the wheelwell that secures the bar in place.

9

The front mounting points are secured using a plate that goes on the underside of the car.

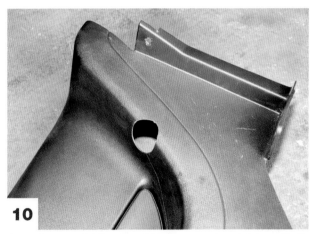

10

The plastic covering that fits on the outside of the rear seats needs to be modified to allow the roll bar to pass through. Use a razor blade or an X-Acto knife to cut a hole where the bar goes through.

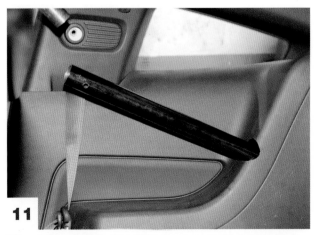

11

With each of the mounting points bolted in, you can remove the bolt that holds the roll bar together and slide the modified plastic covering over the bar to put it back in place.

12

After making sure all of the mounting points are tightly secured, it's time to start replacing the interior trim.

INTERIOR

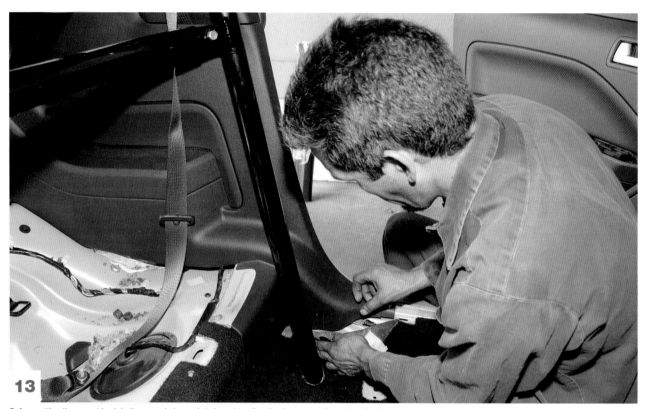

13 Before putting the carpet back in the car, a hole needs to be cut to allow the bar to pass through to the front mounting point.

14 With the interior trim and carpeting back in the car, it's time to put the front seats back into place. If needed, the harness-mount tube can be removed to allow easy access to the rear seats.

INTERIOR

About the Authors

Dan Sanchez has been in the automotive media and aftermarket industry for more than 20 years as a magazine editor, author, and automotive journalist. Sanchez currently is president of DS Media Relations, an advertising/PR/marketing agency and content provider for aftermarket manufacturers and many online and print media. Sanchez is also a well-known author, writer, photographer, and video producer who is called upon by media agencies to provide automotive articles and technical expertise. Much of his recent work has appeared in such magazines as *Mustang Enthusiast, Popular Hot Rodding, Hot Rod, 4Wheel Drive & Sport Utility, Four Wheeler,* and many others. Sanchez currently resides in Corona, California, where he enjoys his 500-plus-horsepower, Kenne Bell–supercharged, 2007 Mustang GT.

Drew Phillips, has been an automotive photojournalist for six years. He is the former editor of *Mustang Life* magazine and is currently working as a full-time freelance automotive photographer and writer. He contributes to such magazines as *5.0 Mustang & Super Fords, Modified Mustang & Fords, Mustang Monthly, Hot Rod,* and *Corvette* magazine. His client list includes Roush and Ford Racing. Phillips' writing and photographs can also be found online at his own website, ModernMustangMuscle.com, and at AutoBlog.com. Drew lives with his wife in Pasadena, California.

Sources

BBK Performance
27440 Bostik Ct.
Temecula, CA 92590
(951) 296-1771
www.bbkperformance.com

Kenne Bell Superchargers
10743 Bell Court
Rancho Cucamonga, CA 91730
(909) 941-6646
www.kennebell.net

Holley Performance Products Inc.
1801 Russellville Road
P.O. Box 10360
Bowling Green, KY 42102
(866) G0-HOLLEY

Snow Performance
1017-A East Hwy 24
Woodland Park, CO 80863
(719) 633-3811
www.SnowPerformance.net

MSD
Autotronic Controls Corporation
1350 Pullman Drive, Dock 14
El Paso, Texas 79936
(915) 857-5200
www.msdignition.com

Brisk USA Enterprises, LLC
133 N. Friendswood Dr., Suite 130
Houston, TX 77546
(713) 459-6977
www.BriskUSA.com
www.BriskRacing.com

Flowmaster
100 Stony Point Road, Suite 125
Santa Rosa, CA 95401
(800) 544-4761
www.flowmastermufflers.com

Moroso
80 Carter Drive
Guilford, CT 06437
(203) 453-6571
www.moroso.com

Diablosport
3500 N. W. Boca Raton Blvd., Suite 504
Boca Raton, FL 33431
(877) 396-6614
www.diablosport.com

APR Performance Inc.
21037 Commerce Pointe Dr.
Walnut, CA 91789
(909) 594-3796
www.aprperformance.com

Shelby Performance Parts LLC
130 Cassia Way
Henderson, NV 89014
(702) 405-3500
www.shelbyperformanceparts.com

Vogtland North America
43391 Business Park Dr., Suite C10
Temecula, CA 92590
(951) 694-6981
www.vogtland-na.com

Tokico
475 Alaska Ave
Torrance, CA 90503
(310) 212-0200
www.tokicogasshocks.com

Pure Motorsport
41740 Enterprise Circle N., Suite 108
Temecula, CA 92590
(866) 397-5487
www.purems.com

Whiteline Automotive
Global Performance Parts
4554 128th Ave.
Holland, MI 49424
(616) 399-9025
www.GlobalPerformanceParts.com

BMR Fabrication
12581 US Highway 301 N
Thonotosassa, FL 33592
(813) 986-9302
www.bmrfabrication.com

J Bittle American Performance Center
5135 Convoy St.
San Diego, CA 92111
(888) 522-5570
www.jbaracing.com

JBA Performance Center
5135 Convoy St.
San Diego, CA 92111
(888) 522-5570
www.jbaracing.com

Granatelli Motorsports
1000 Yarnell Place
Oxnard, CA 93033
(804) 466-6644
www.granatellimotorsports.com

Baer Inc.
3108 W. Thomas Rd., Suite 1201-Q
Phoenix, AZ 85017
(602) 233-1411
www.baer.com

Toyo Tires USA
6261 Katella Ave., Suite 2B
Cypress, CA 90630
(800) 678-3250
www.toyo.com

Centerforce Clutches
2266 Crosswind Drive.
Prescott, AZ 86301
(928) 771-8422
www.centerforce.com

TCI Automotive
151 Industrial Drive
Ashland, MS 38603
(888) 776-9824
www.tciauto.com

Street Scene Equipment
365 McCormick Avenue
Costa Mesa, CA 92626
(714) 426-0590
www.streetsceneeq.com

A-1 Auto Body
825 North Andreason Dr. #C
Escondido, CA 92029
(760) 839-0404

Classic Design Concepts LLC
42860 W. Nine Mile Rd.
Novi, MI 48375
(866) 624-7997
www.classicdesignconcepts.com

Agent 47
2221 Rutherford Rd.
Carlsbad, CA 92008
(760) 496-3809
www.agentfourtyseven.com

Speed of Sound LLC
www.speedofsoundllc.com
(866) 48-GAUGE

Autometer Products Inc.
413 West Elm Street
Sycamore, IL 60178
(866) 248-6356
www.autometer.com

Autopower Industries
3424 Pickett St.
San Diego, CA 92110
(619) 297-3300
www.autopowerindustries.com

Index

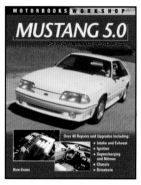